Embracing the Exotic

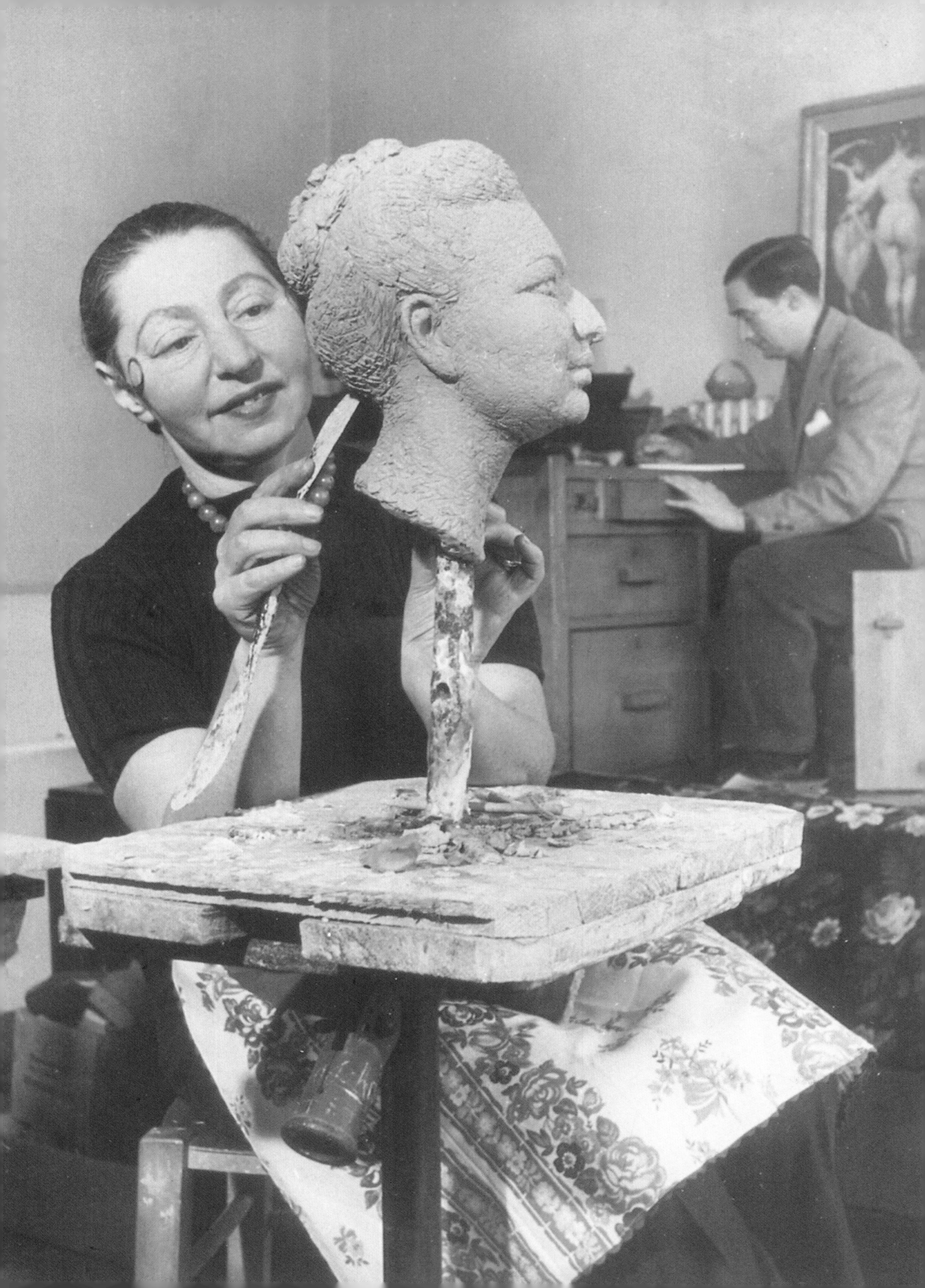

Embracing the Exotic

Jacob Epstein & Dora Gordine

Ben Uri Gallery, The London Jewish Museum of Art

10 January – 19 March 2006

Hatton Gallery, University of Newcastle

27 March – 20 May 2006

KINGSTON UNIVERSITY

HATTON GALLERY

The Henry Moore Foundation

REGISTERED MUSEUM

MUSEUMS ASSOCIATION INSTITUTIONAL MEMBER

3 1/2 centuries of british jewish life

Jews were welcomed by Cromwell in 1656. Throughout 2006, we pay special tribute to their heritage, presence and future in Britain.

350@bod.org.uk

aejm association of european jewish museums

Ben Uri Gallery

The London Jewish Museum of Art

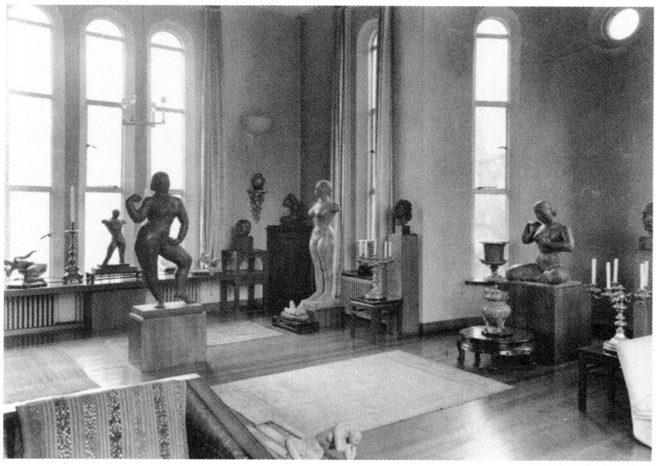 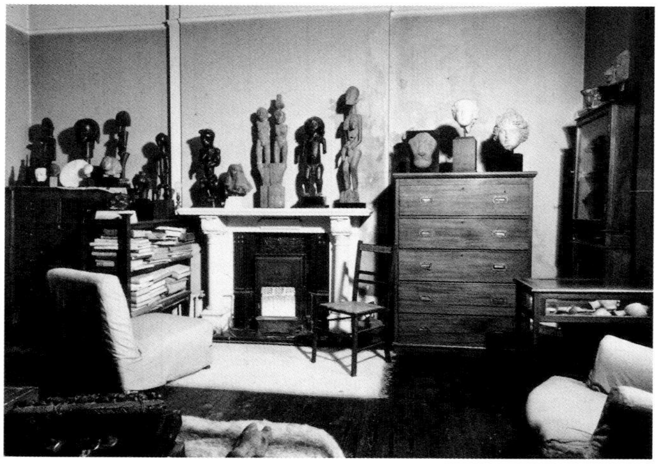

front cover: (cat no. 11) Jacob Epstein, *Study for Man-Woman,* 1913
back cover: (cat no. 36) Dora Gordine, *Malay Head,* 1930-35
frontis: (Fig. 1) *Dora Gordine at work with Richard Hare in the background,* c.1948
above left: *The Gallery at Dorich House*, c.1955
above right: Geoffrey Ireland, *Bedroom at Hyde Park Gate showing famous Fang Head and Dogon Mother and Child*, c. 1959

Edited by Sarah MacDougall and Rachel Dickson
Design director: Alexandra Papadakis

First published in Great Britain in 2006 by
PAPADAKIS PUBLISHER
An imprint of New Architecture Group Limited
16 Grosvenor Place, London SW1X 7HH

In association with
Ben Uri Gallery, The London Jewish Museum of Art

ISBN 1 901092 63 1

Printed and bound in Singapore

Contents

To inspire, to connect, to make a difference

Ben Uri Gallery, The London Jewish Museum of Art

Ben Uri Gallery, founded in 1915, is Europe's only dedicated Jewish Museum of Art, working in partnership with secular and Jewish Museums in the United Kingdom and internationally. The Ben Uri Gallery and Museum is an educational institution dedicated to enhancing the quality of life of all whom it impacts. It believes in and embraces a wider role for museums in society today and is unafraid to address contemporary issues through exhibitions and outreach programmes. It is committed to demonstrating the virtues of Art as a bridge between peoples and their beliefs.

Its purpose is to enable the largest possible audience, drawn from the widest possible communities from both home and abroad, to explore for inspiration, learning and enjoyment, the work, lives and contribution of British and European artists of Jewish descent, placed where relevant alongside their non-Jewish contemporaries, within the artistic and social context of the national cultural heritage.

Its principal route to achieving this is by enabling broad, easy and straightforward physical and visual access – through location, publication and internet outreach – to the following:

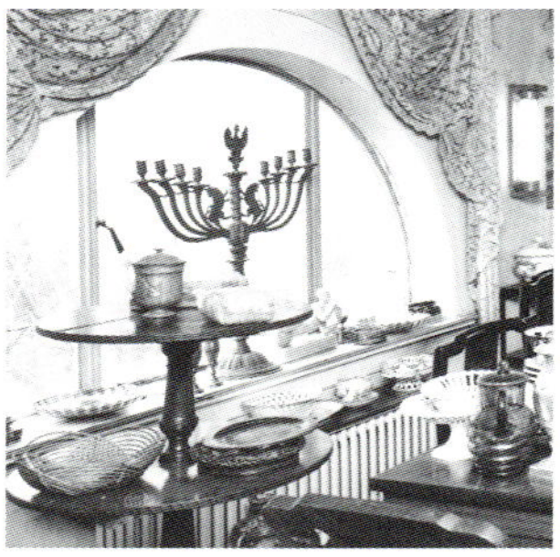

Fig 2 **Detail from the Dining Room at Dorich House with Menorah**, c.1949

The Permanent Collection
The largest of its kind in the world, accessed physically or virtually via continued exhibition, research, conservation and acquisition.

Temporary Exhibitions
Curating, touring and hosting important internationally-focused exhibitions of the widest artistic appeal that, without the museum's focus, would not be seen in the United Kingdom.

Publications
Commissioning new academic research on the artists and their historical context to accompany the museum's exhibitions.

Library and Archive
A resource dating from the turn of the 20th century, documenting and tracing in parallel the artistic and social development of the Ben Uri and Jewish artists working or exhibiting in Britain, alongside and as part of the evolving British historical landscape.

Education Programmes
For adults, students, school children and artists, through symposia, lectures, student packs, visits and artist peer group programmes.

Artists
Monthly Artist Peer Group Programmes, Ben Uri International Jewish Artists of the Year Awards competition, Guidance and affiliation benefits.

Care in the Community
Through the pioneering pilot project between the Ben Uri and the British Association of Art Therapists.

Website
Providing an on-line educational and access tool, to function as a virtual gallery and artists' reference resource for students, collectors and scholars.

3 1/2 centuries of british jewish life

Ben Uri Gallery

The London Jewish Museum of Art

Chairman's Foreword

As we move through the early years of this new century, the role of the museum and gallery becomes ever more complex and diverse. If galleries and museums are to succeed in broadening their appeal and in attracting new visitors from outside the expected and established audience pools, the formula must revolve primarily around issues of 'relevance' and 'connection'.

Embracing the Exotic focuses its scholarship on the effect of non-western influences on the oeuvre of two very different sculptors, both immigrants to this country, over seventy years ago – the first time this has been documented and supported by an exhibition of this breadth and depth. However, there is also an underlying social dimension that has significant relevance today in a changed London and in a changed world.

We sincerely hope that in hosting this exhibition, Ben Uri not only adds new academe to the knowledge of the work and influences of two great sculptors, but also stimulates debate on how we, in our rich multi-cultural and multi-ethnic society, can encourage the growth and integration of new cultural identities into the mainstream national identity.

The Ben Uri Gallery has a distinguished history of hosting exhibitions by Sir Jacob Epstein (1880-1959), one of the most significant figures in twentieth century British sculpture, including *Sir Jacob Epstein, 1880-1950: exhibition of bronzes*, held posthumously in 1959, and *Epstein centenary 1980: bronzes, drawings and watercolours*. It therefore gives me great pleasure that the Ben Uri is now originating and touring the first major exhibition to compare the work of Epstein with that of his lesser-known female contemporary, Dora Gordine (1898-1991), herself the subject of new research. Comprising sculpture, drawing and ethnographic pieces, the exhibition seeks to critically examine how both figures were inspired by non-western cultures and how they came to make such a significant impact on the development of Modern British sculpture.

We are also delighted that the Hatton Gallery, University of Newcastle, will be hosting the second leg of the exhibition, as touring is one of the Ben Uri's key exhibition objectives. As owner of the Ullman Ethnographic Collection, the Hatton is a most fitting second venue.

We are indebted to the eminent art historian and critic, Richard Cork; Dr Jonathan Black, AHRB Fellow at Dorich House; Brenda Martin, Curator, Dorich House, and Victor Arwas, art historian, gallerist and collector, for their scholarly contributions to the catalogue. We are extremely grateful to internationally renowned sculptor, Sir Anthony Caro, for his insightful introduction, and to Dr Suzanne Ullman, Geoffrey Ireland and Betty Peterson, whose recollections of these two extraordinary sculptors add a vital and personal dimension to the catalogue.

I would also like to thank all our lenders, both public and private, in readily making works accessible to us. Particular thanks are due to Dorich House who have made their new research on Gordine so freely available, and have been extremely generous with the loan of her works, some of which have not been seen in public for a generation or more. We are also grateful for the generosity and assistance of Jo Digger at the New Art Gallery Walsall, home to the Garman Ryan Collection, who has lent both Epstein works and a number of significant ethnographic pieces to this exhibition. Other loans are drawn from notable national and regional collections including Tate, British Museum, National Museums and Galleries of Wales, Leeds City Art Gallery, Henry Moore Centre for the Study of Sculpture, Nottingham Castle Museum and Gallery and Birmingham Museum and Art Galleries.

The Ben Uri does not benefit from any public funding and is reliant on the generous financial support of our Friends group and many charitable foundations. We are indebted to all our exhibition sponsors, including many private supporters We particularly thank The Henry Moore Foundation, which is supporting the Ben Uri for the first time, for financial assistance with the exhibition; The Paul Mellon Centre for Studies in British Art, for supporting the catalogue; and a private patron of the arts, for honouring both. Without these contributions this endeavour would not have been possible. We are also grateful to Hanadiv Charitable Foundation and The Dorset Trust Foundation for their ongoing support of the Ben Uri.

Finally, we pay tribute to the dedication, energy and scholarship of our curators, Rachel Dickson and Sarah MacDougall.

Please enjoy the exhibition and take with you the thought of how we, in Britain, can best continue the tradition of welcoming new influences into our national cultural heritage, as Epstein and Gordine 'Embraced the Exotic' over seventy years ago.

David J Glasser
Chairman

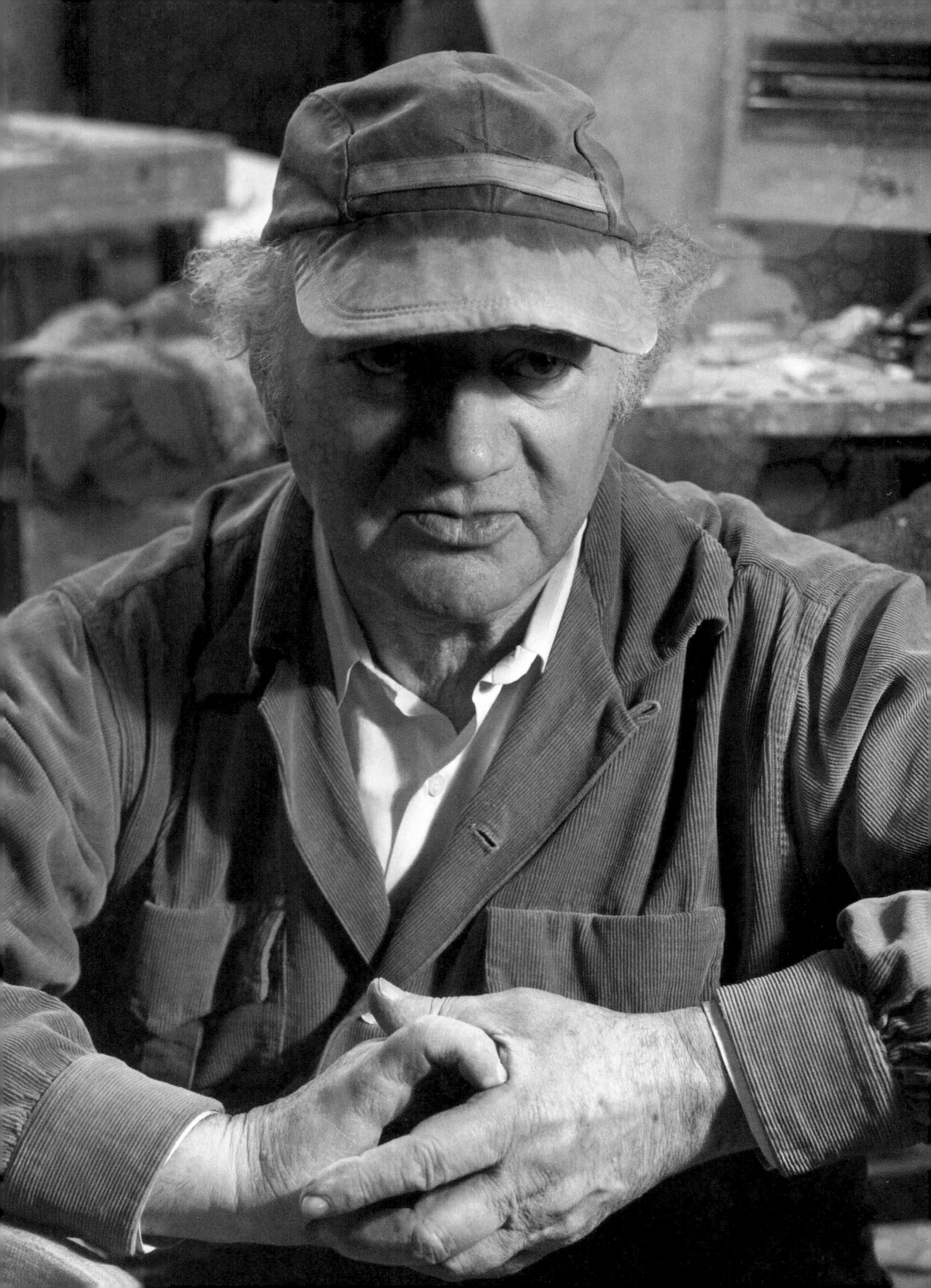

Curators' Introduction

Fig. 3 **Jacob Epstein,** 1953
Photo: Ida Kar

Embracing the Exotic: Jacob Epstein and Dora Gordine is the fifth exhibition in the Ben Uri's ongoing series 'Whitechapel Boys', which examines the contribution of the group of Anglo-Jewish artists, all born, raised or working in London's East End in the first decades of the twentieth century, and who made a significant impact on twentieth-century British art and a particular contribution to British Modernism. This exhibition broadens the series' remit to focus on sculpture as a medium and on the work of a female artist. Furthermore, it is the first exhibition to examine in detail the impact of 'Primitive' art upon these two modern British sculptors.

In realising this exhibition we have had the opportunity to deal with a number of curatorial challenges: firstly, to compare Epstein with a female contemporary sculptor (which has never been done before) – a fellow émigré, almost certainly Jewish, whose own 'exotic' background was deliberately self-obscured – and, secondly, to examine how both artists were drawn, in very different ways, to the non-European model for inspiration.

Previous exhibitions, such as the much debated *Primitivism in 20th Century Art: Affinity of the Tribal and Modern* (New York, MOMA, 1984), and Silber and Friedman's important *Jacob Epstein: Sculpture and Drawings* (Leeds and London, 1987) have done much to highlight the wide-ranging debates surrounding the 'Primitive' and Modern art. However, by pairing Epstein and Gordine for the first time, this exhibition offers scope for a significant contribution to the current debates surrounding the nature of identity, by placing the non-western influence within the wider context of British colonialism and attitudes to the 'other' in the early part of the twentieth century.

Epstein and Gordine make a fascinating pairing. At the height of their careers, they were both showing work at the prestigious and forward-looking Leicester Galleries, London; both were founder members of the Society of Portrait Sculptors, and both came to the attention of significant English collectors of modern art, such as Sir Michael Sadler. Indeed, their names were first coupled by the critic R H Wilenski in the *Evening Standard* following Gordine's very first London showing at the Leicester Galleries in October 1928.[i] The following November when a group exhibition of *Modern and African Sculpture* opened at the Sydney Burney Gallery in London, the 'Moderns' included the first sculptural pairing of Epstein and Gordine, their work placed alongside carvings from Dahomey, Gabon, Nigeria, Benin and the Congo.[ii] This suggested not only their artistic connection, but also highlighted the perceived exoticism of both their backgrounds, as well as their shared interest in non-western subject matter. Four years later, when, together with Maillol, they were also both included in a summer group exhibition of *Drawings, Paintings and Sculpture by Modern Artists* at the Leicester Galleries – where Gordine's three works included *Dahomey Princess* – this common interest in non-western (and here specifically African) subjects, was no longer merely suggested but proven. Over the next thirty years, their work would be shown together in group shows on at least six further occasions.

By 1949 E H Ramsden in *Twentieth Century Sculpture*, was classing both as adept portrayers of 'oriental personalities'; probably pairing them because of their supposed shared origins: Gordine is described as 'Russian-born' while Epstein is very clearly identified as of 'Russian-Polish origin'. The underlying implication behind such labeling appears to be that both are foreign (probably Jewish) and therefore automatically attracted by 'oriental' subject matter. The critic Herbert Furst, in reviewing the exhibition of Epstein's *Seventy Five Drawings* (cat no. 51), which were mostly nude studies of Epstein's Indian models, the sisters Anita and Sunita, drew attention to the artist's preference for "Oriental – Jewish, Indian and exotic – negroid feminity –", but concluded "*chacun à son goût*. That surely is his affair." [iii]

Epstein, a Jewish émigré, never made any secret of his Jewishness, and his own perceived 'exoticism' clashed with prevailing British attitudes, although, as Victor Arwas suggests in his essay, anti-Semitism was probably at the root of much of the hostile reaction to Epstein's public work.[iv] Gordine, though she never stated her religion, was widely assumed to be Jewish by her friends and supporters, such as D S MacColl and Lucien Pissarro, and she is known to have kept a *Menorah* at Dorich House. Yet, the very fluidity of Gordine's identity (was she Latvian, Estonian or Russian by birth and why was she so keen to embrace British

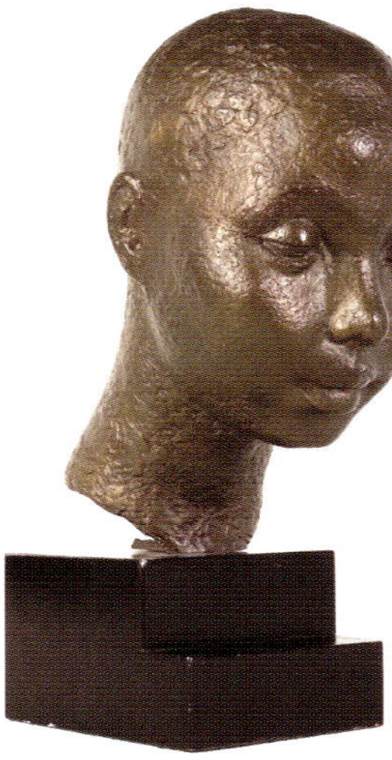

33 Dora Gordine
African Head, 1929

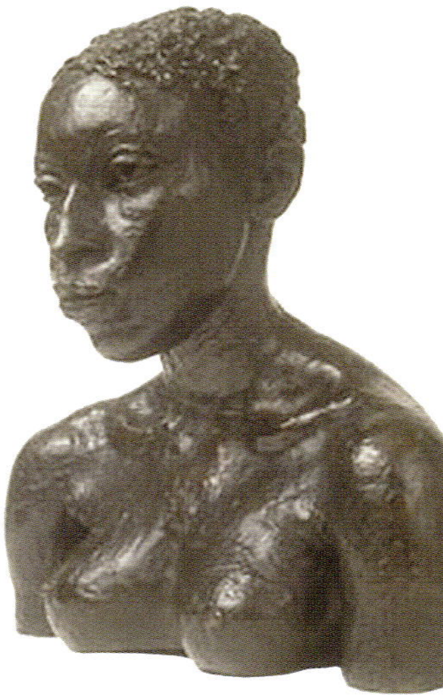

22 Jacob Epstein
Second Portrait of Lydia, 1931

citizenship?) intrigued the critics and the many admirers of her work within the British cultural establishment. And, as both Jonathan Black and Brenda Martin reveal in their essays, her self-created 'exoticism' – with her Jewishness if not hidden then certainly not openly acknowledged – actually helped to establish her reputation in Britain.

Furthermore, throughout their working lives, both sculptors sought to establish and surround themselves with their own highly personal 'exotic' collections, which in turn had a significant effect on their work. Epstein built up one of the finest and earliest ethnographic collections in England during the early part of the twentieth century, inspiring fellow Jewish artists such as Jacob Kramer and Joseph Herman to follow his lead. Upon Epstein's death this collection numbered almost a thousand pieces and included works whose origins were as diverse as Africa, Oceania, India and Egypt.

Both sculptors were fascinated by the Ancient civilisations of India, China and Egypt, sharing a particular interest in the latter. Both revered and wrote about the sandstone *Mask of Nefertiti* in the Berlin Museum and Epstein also owned an Egyptian plaster female mask (cat no. 47), which he believed to be a cast of the Ancient Egyptian queen. Both also experimented with the mask form: Gordine in her classic *Mask of a Greek Boy* (1929, cat no. 34) and Epstein in his Indian-inspired *Third Portrait of Meum (Mask)* (1918, cat no. 14).

The immense visual power of these pieces is evidenced in the haunting black-and-white photographs taken of the collection in the 1950s by Epstein's photographer, Geoffrey Ireland, a number of which, along with Ireland's fascinating account of how this enterprise came about, are reproduced in this catalogue.

Equally, the importance of the collection as a whole was confirmed in the 1960 Arts Council exhibition and catalogue, *The Epstein collection of tribal and exotic sculpture*, with an introduction by the British Museum's renowned ethnographic expert, William Fagg. Dispersed posthumously, much of the collection has, appropriately, found its way into important public collections, most notably the British Museum itself.[v] Yet as Fagg himself observed elsewhere, Epstein's 'admiration for his African or Polynesian masterpieces' and his 'use of the African form was entirely transmuted to his own artistic purpose.'[vi]

African art lay at the heart of Epstein's collection and although he denied any specific influence, he admired in it 'characteristics that are far removed from our traditional European rendering of form in Greek, in Gothic, or in Renaissance traditions'.[vii] How potent this influence was can also be traced in Epstein's early portraits of one of his favourite models, Nan Condron, a young woman of Gypsy origin and a professional model, whom he had discovered at London's Café Royal. In a series of studies of Nan, c.1909-12, Epstein's early naturalism gave way to increasingly stylised representations, notably in *Nan Condron as the Brummer Head* (1913, Fig. 27) as his excitement and interest in his ethnographic collection grew and became 'not only a source of delight and contentment for him, but also a repertory of sculptural forms, of solutions to the problem of representing the human figure or head'.[viii]

Despite works like *Dahomey Princess* and her delicate female *African Head* (1929, cat no. 33), which forms part of the exploration of different racial characters by the artist during the late 1920s, and was

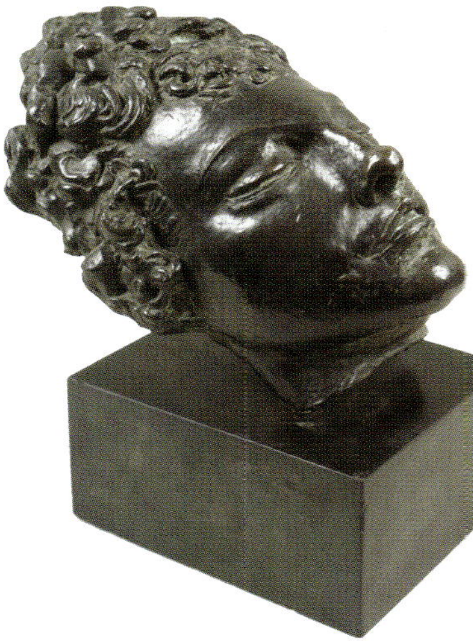

14 Jacob Epstein
Third Portrait of Meum (Mask), 1918

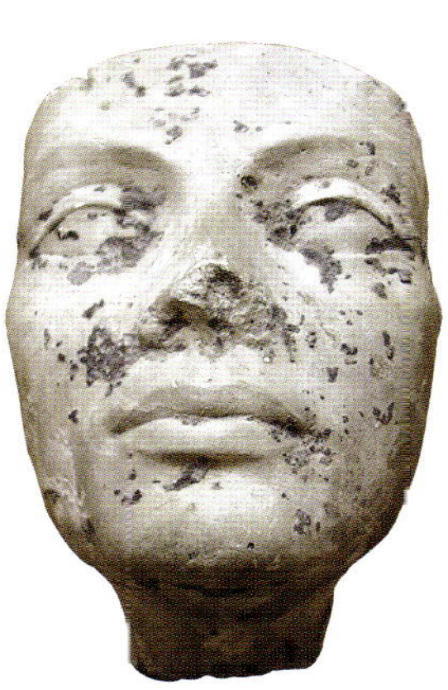

47 *Mask of Nefertiti* (Egyptian),
1350-1300 BC

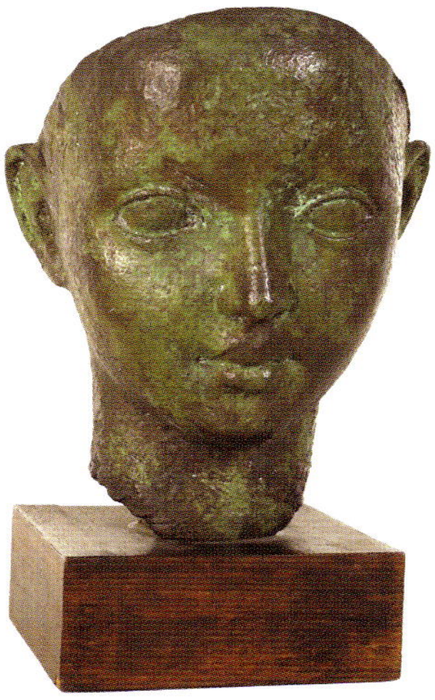

34 Dora Gordine
Mask of a Greek Boy, 1929

43 Dora Gordine
Seated Oriental Woman with Arms Raised, 1930-35

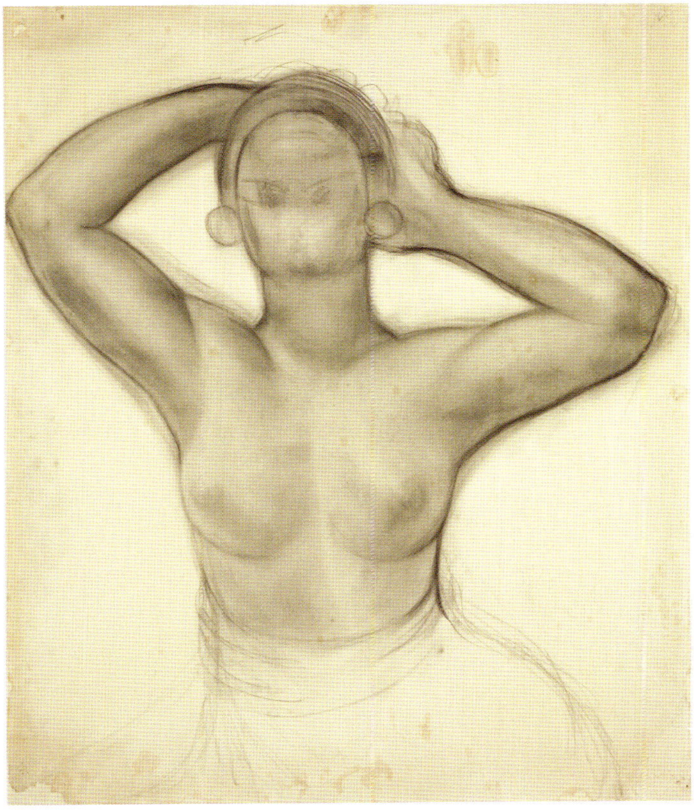

20 Jacob Epstein
Sunita, c.1930

23 Jacob Epstein
Indian Mother and Child, c.1932

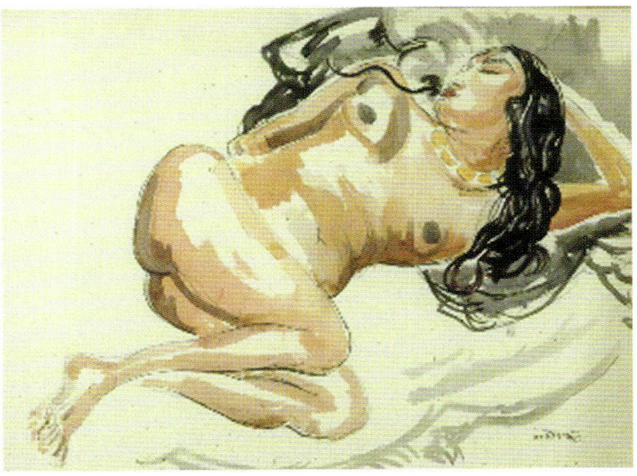

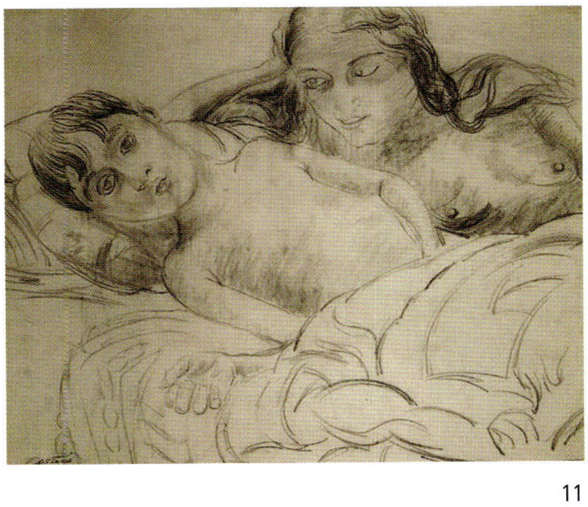

right:
31 Dora Gordine
Baby's Head, 1928

far right:

Fig. 4 Jacob Epstein
Baby Awake, 1902-4
Catalogue only

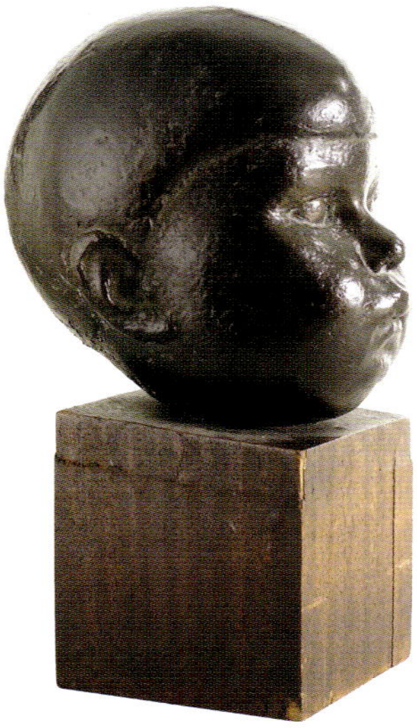

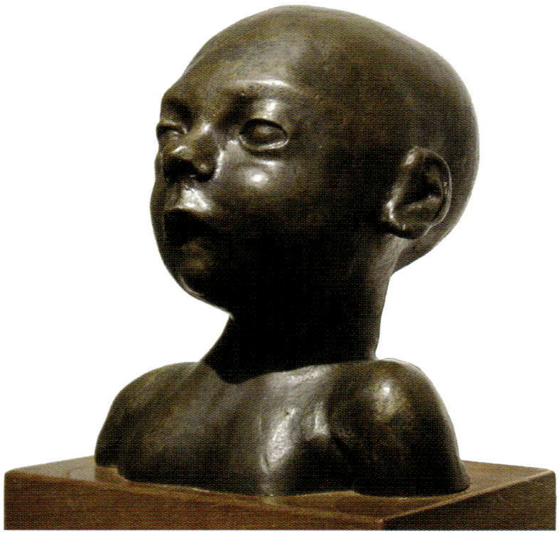

bought for the Municipal Buildings in Singapore, Gordine's inspiration remained firmly rooted in the East. Photographic records show that, before her death, she amassed a large personal collection of Ancient Eastern Art, which, though since dispersed, clearly had a formative influence on her own work. Gordine, together with her aristocratic, academic husband, Richard Hare, also collected Russian *objets d'art*, and they specifically designed and built their Modernist home, Dorich House, now magnificently restored as part of Kingston University, to house this collection. Although Russian art did not directly influence her sculpture, Gordine used her collection as a striking backdrop against which to display and enhance her own carefully nurtured exoticism. Dr Suzanne Ullman, a lifelong friend of Gordine's, also recalls in her personal memoir of Gordine that the Hares led a distinctly frugal life in order to sustain their collection, and hoped to leave it to the nation after their deaths.

Both sculptors, at least initially, gained inspiration from Europe and its acknowledged artistic capital: Paris. Between 1909-12, Epstein's contact there with Brancusi and Modigliani stimulated his revival of direct-carving, and this combined with the impact of the 'exotic' radically transformed his style in these crucial years, in works such as the stone carving, *Rom* (1910, cat no. 6), which the critic C Lewis Hind described as 'the Eternal Child that has crowed and capered from Egypt and Assyria to the present moment'[ix]. Gordine, too, took influence from Paris: encouraged by Maillol, she launched her career there and *Javanese Dancer* (1927, cat no. 30) shows how strongly she absorbed his influence. She also first exhibited her work in Paris in 1925, and in 1929 commissioned the French architect Auguste Perret to design a Modernist studio home for her in the artists' quarter of Boulogne-Billancourt.

Yet there are a number of very significant differences between these two sculptors, not least in their methods. Epstein worked both as a modeller and a carver, while Gordine worked exclusively as a modeller, concentrating on the patina of her surfaces to produce striking effects. Comparison of the two works: Epstein's *Second Portrait of Lydia* (1931, cat no. 22) and Gordine's *African Head* demonstrates that while Epstein was concerned with modelling the characteristics of the individual, Gordine sought often to express a generic, often asexual, neither overtly male nor female, 'type'.

In contrast, Epstein's work is dominated by his enduring interest in themes of sexuality, fertility, birth and motherhood, which suggest that he saw a direct relationship between the artist's creativity and female fecundity. These themes are explored in a number of pieces in the exhibition, ranging from the early pencil *Study for Figure of Maternity* (c.1910, cat no. 7) to the raw power of Epstein's *Genesis* (1929-30, Fig. 6); see also *Genesis II* (1929-30, cat no. 19), a work that Epstein himself described as: 'the deep down instinctive female, without the trapping and charm of what is known as feminine...'[x] Elsewhere, the important double funerary sculpture from Madagascar (Fig. 21. *Architectural carving in form of male and female figure, Madagascar*) influenced Epstein's outstanding double-figure drawing *Study for Man-Woman* (1913, cat no. 11) now housed, appropriately, alongside several of his own ethnographic pieces, in the British Museum. Later, in his seminal readymade *Rock Drill* (c.19913, cat no. 13), Epstein would invert the idea of female fertility by using a male, angular and non-organic figure in place

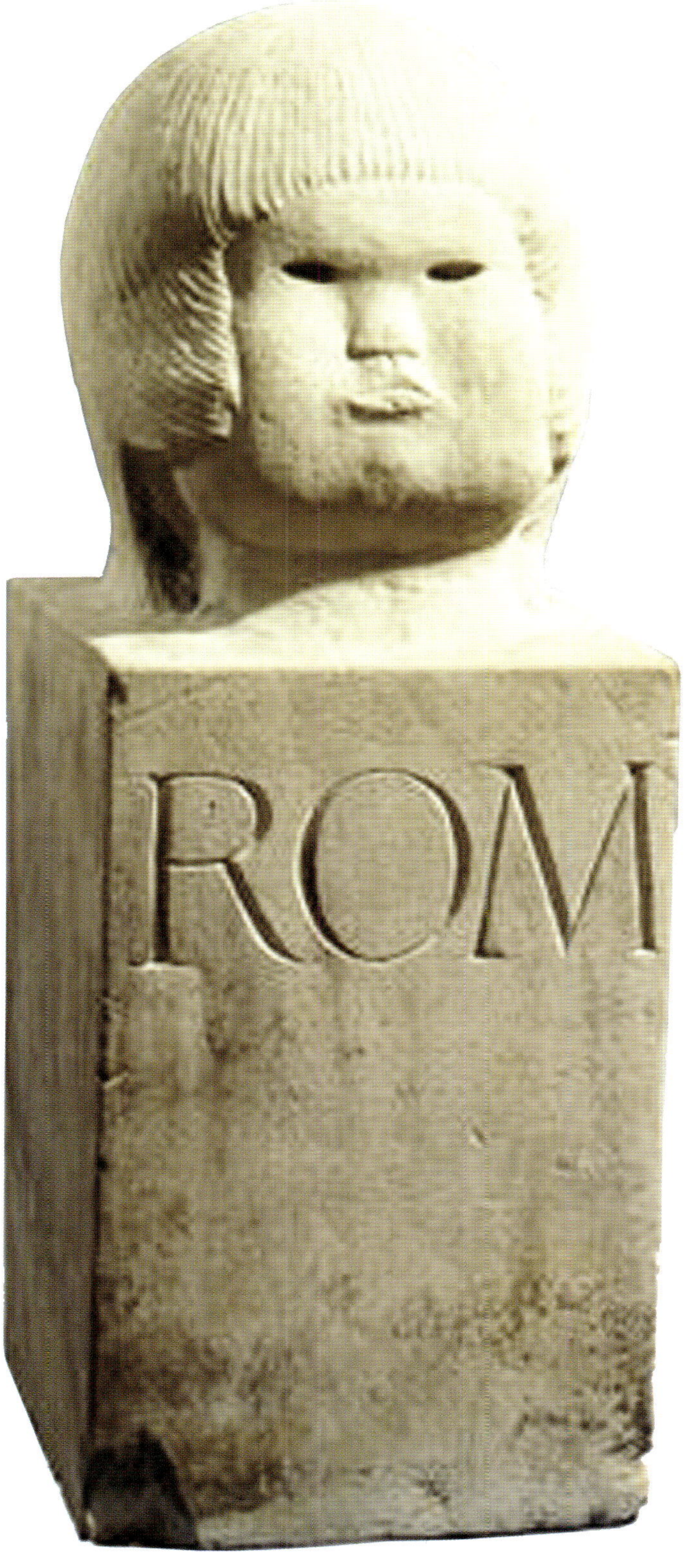

6 Jacob Epstein
Rom, 1910

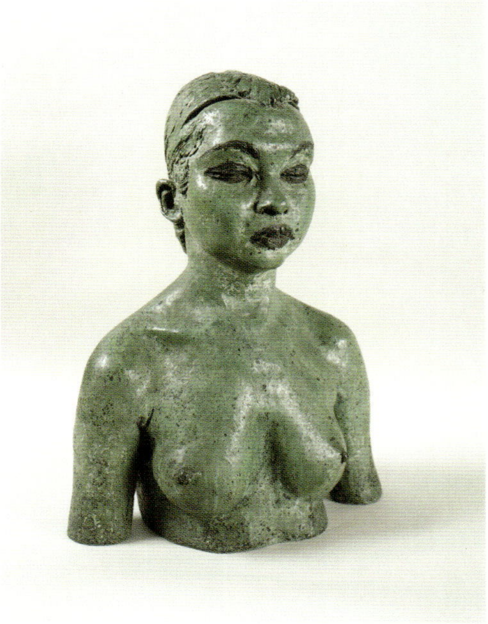

24 Jacob Epstein
Rani Rama, 1934

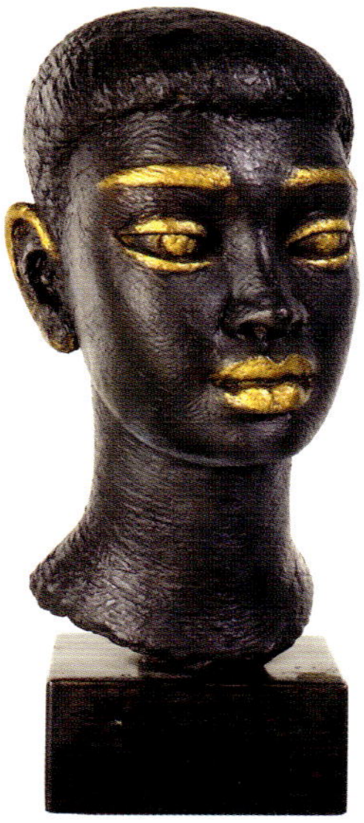

46 Dora Gordine
Black Orchid

1 Jacob Epstein
Self-Portrait, 1901

of a voluptuous, nurturing female type, to express the sterile impotence of the new machine age.

Sexuality, so important in Epstein's work, rarely breaks through in Gordine. Though claiming that her sculptures were her children,[xi] Gordine failed to explore this theme actively in her work, though the sinuous grace of her pastel-and-crayon studies of oriental women, such as *Seated Oriental Woman with Arms Raised* (1930-35, cat no. 43), suggests a gentle sensuality not wholly removed from Epstein's studies of Sunita and her child, Enver (*Indian Mother and Child*, c. 1932, cat no 23). Although never a mother herself, Gordine certainly sculpted children; indeed, her *Baby's Head* (1928, cat no. 31) shows an unmistakable resemblance to both Epstein's *Rom* and *Baby Awake* (Fig. 4). But her substantial female nudes, particularly *Pagan* (Fig. 13) and *Javanese Dancer*, like Maillol's famous *Pomona*, are no more than suggestive of female fecundity.

In conclusion, by juxtaposing works by these two sculptors alongside a number of Epstein's own ethnographic pieces, we hope that this exhibition will raise many rich and complex issues about the individual, identity and the nature of sculpture, which resonate as much in today's multicultural society as they did in Britain some seventy years ago. We also hope that this Ben Uri exhibition about two very different émigré sculptors is a fitting opening to the yearlong cultural celebration to mark three and a half centuries of British Jewish life.

Sarah MacDougall and Rachel Dickson

[i] *Evening Standard*, 5 October 1928, cited Jonathan Black, *A Genius for the Exotic: Dora Gordine, Imperialism and the Racial Type in Portraiture*, in *Embracing the Exotic: Jacob Epstein and Dora Gordine* (London: Ben Uri Gallery, The London Jewish Museum of Art, in association with Papadakis Publisher, 2006), p.37

[ii] Other exhibitors included Ossip Zadkine, Aristide Maillol, Barbara Hepworth, John Skeaping and Frank Dobson

[iii] Frank Felsenstein, "Epstein as Book Illustrator 1900-1940", *Jacob Epstein: Sculpture and Drawings* (Leeds: Maney in association with the Henry Moore Centre for the Study of Sculpture,1987, republished 1989), p.199

[iv] See also Elizabeth Barker "The Primitive Within: The Question of Race in Epstein's Career 1917-1929" in Silber and Friedman, op. cit.

[v] See Ezio Bassani and Malcolm McLeod in *Jacob Epstein, Collector* (Milan, 1989) and "The Passionate Collector", Silber and Friedman, op. cit.

[vi] William Fagg, *African and New Guinea sculpture from the Josef Herman Collection: paintings and drawings by Josef Herman,* (Edinburgh: Scottish National Gallery of Modern Art, 1969), unpaginated

[vii] Jacob Epstein, *Let There Be Sculpture: The Autobiography of Jacob Epstein* (London: Michael Joseph,1940); this edition, New York: Arno Press, 1975, p.188

[viii] E Bassani and M McLeod, "A Passionate Collector", Silber and Friedman, op. cit., p.12

[ix] C L Hind, *The Post-Impressionists* (London: Methuen, 1911), pp.66-7, cited E Silber *The Sculpture of Epstein with a Complete Catalogue* (Oxford: Phaidon Press, 1986), pp.126-7

x Evelyn Silber and Terry Friedman, "Isolation and Defiance 1930-1943", Silber and Friedman, op. cit., p.230

[xi] *Dora Gordine Sculpture Collection, Dorich House Museum, Kingston University*, (Dorset: Bond & Coyne, 2005), p.7

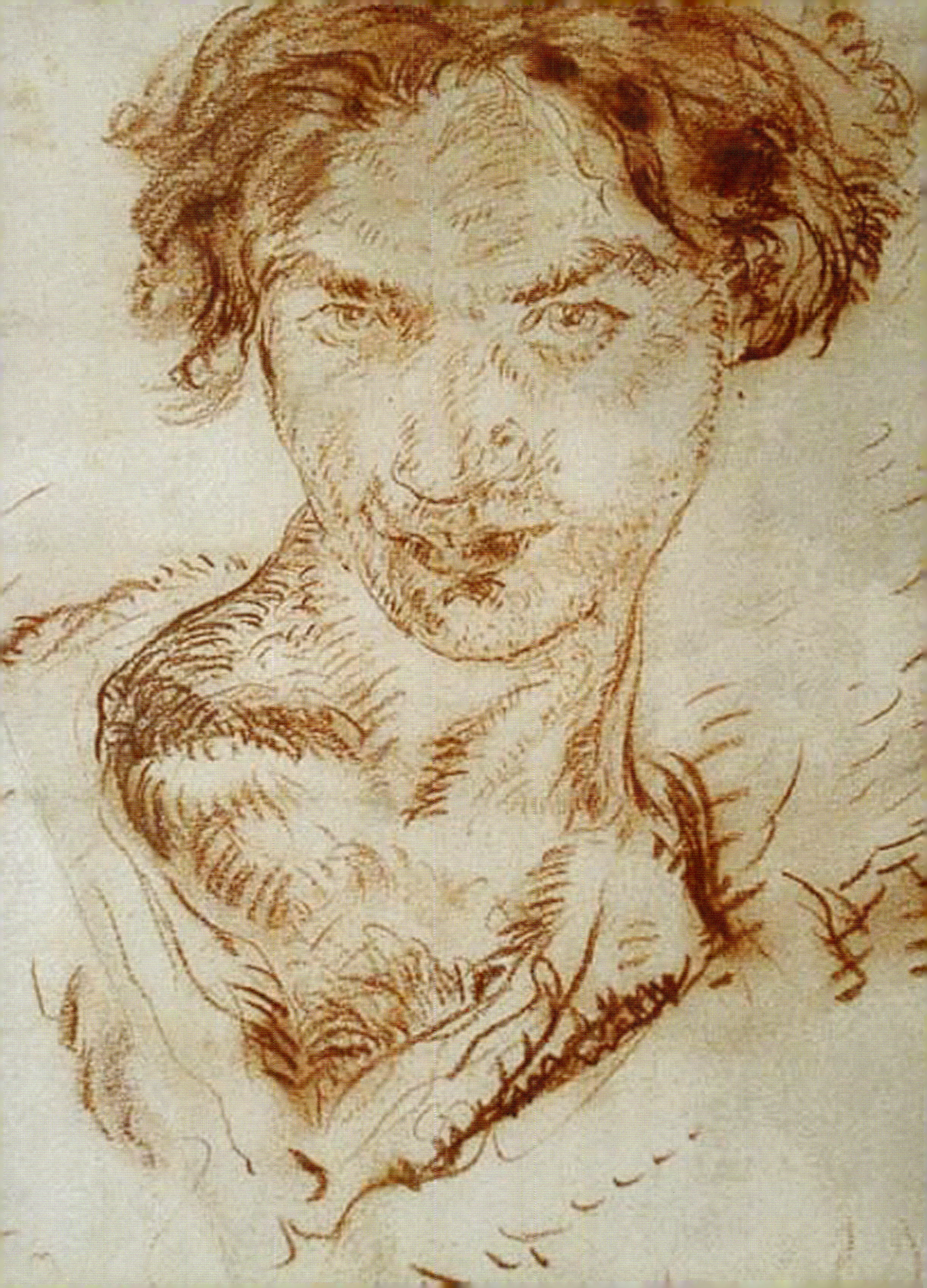

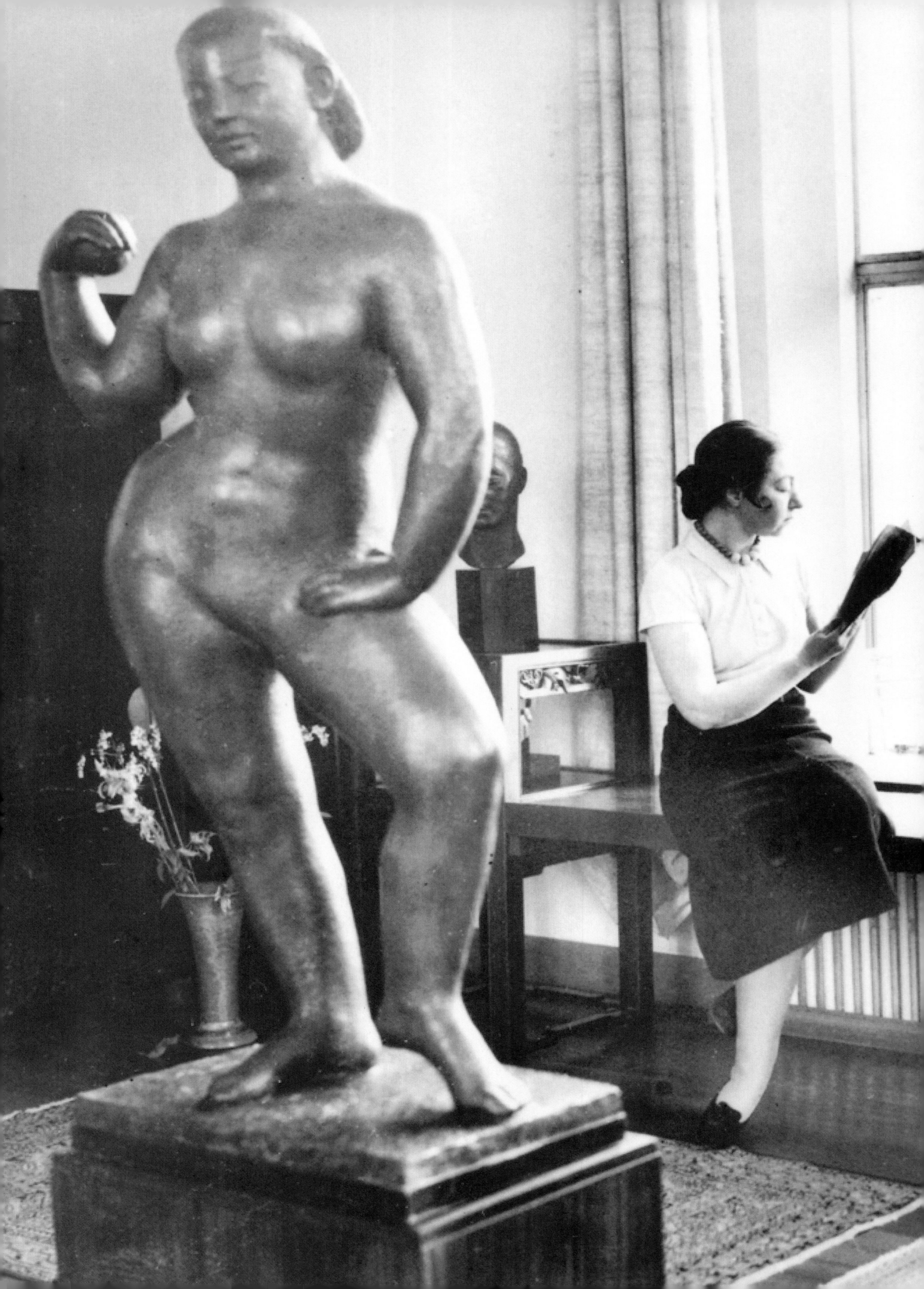

Introduction by Sir Anthony Caro

When I first began to study sculpture, the English artists that we looked to were Jacob Epstein and Dora Gordine. In the 1940s Henry Moore's work was not known at all to us students. Each of these sculptors had taken decisive steps away from academia and the influence of Greek and Roman art; they looked instead at African, Mexican or Indian sculpture. They had realised that what had been the way forward since the Renaissance was no longer open to them but that going forward meant looking elsewhere. It was Negro art that had sparked Picasso's revolution in painting a decade or so earlier: now it was the turn of sculpture.

Epstein led the way – Moore used to pay tribute to him for taking the first steps and indeed for taking the brunt of the opposition in the early days. His *Rock Drill* of 1913-15, his stone carvings, *Jacob and the Angel, Day and Night*, are marvellous, powerful, forward-looking sculptures. They display great emotional strength but by the 1940s they had had their moment and were no longer seen in public places. Instead they were either in store forgotten, or even in one case, shown on a pier as a funfair item. He was never able to bring the strength of his early carvings into his later commissioned groups. However the freshness of his vision had changed sculpture. Epstein had been forced to work largely as a portrait artist and his connection with the Vorticists and the new in French art seems to have been severed.

His bronze portrait busts show what a superb portraitist and modeller he was; every one has character, some are magnificent. In them he tried to see through to the elemental force of nature and not to be seduced by eroticism or prettiness.

Dora Gordine never had the wildness or taste for experimentation of Epstein, but she was an ambitious artist and her work has strength. It is clear that she looked at Indian art and her sculpture has a serenity, a steadiness. She had the good sense to look to Maillol and her art is withheld, slowed down, as is the art of Maillol. It may not seem so very extraordinary to us nowadays, but when we place her work against that of the much more successful academic sculptors of the time it is a million miles better.

Epstein and Gordine had a vision of the promised land. Like all the artists who have turned their eyes towards primitive cultures, they began by copying the style that had turned them on. Picasso and Moore both did this, but eventually the lessons of the primitive get developed to create a new kind of art. This was the step that neither Epstein nor Gordine was able to take. Had they had the backing, the critical response, their undoubted sculptural strength and sensitivity would in all probability have changed the history of sculpture in this country. The revolution in sculpture might have taken place thirty years earlier and might have led in very different directions. As it is, we salute the work of two excellent artists, makers of fine, strong sculptures: we owe them our respect. They are our sculptural ancestors and they cracked the mould.

Summer 2005

Fig. 5 Dora Gordine at home, c.1939

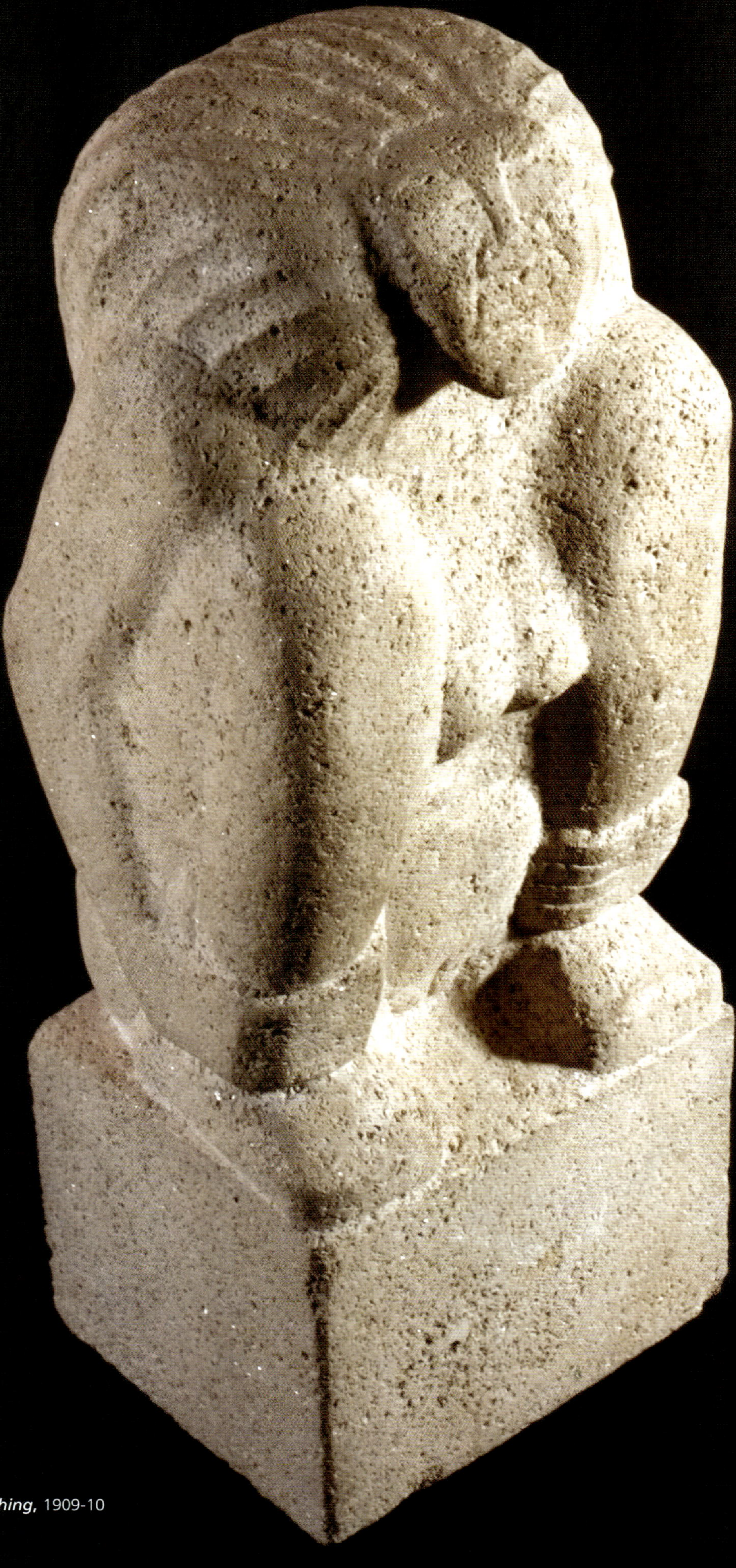

4 Jacob Epstein
Sun Goddess, Crouching, 1909-10

Epstein's Carvings and Non-Western Cultures

Richard Cork

Richard Cork is an art critic, historian, broadcaster and exhibition organiser. He has been Art Critic of the *London Evening Standard*, Editor of *Studio International*, Art Critic of *The Listener*, Chief Art Critic of *The Times* and Art Critic of *The New Statesman*. A frequent broadcaster on radio and television, he has organised major contemporary and historical exhibitions at the Tate Gallery, the Royal Academy, the Hayward Gallery and elsewhere in Europe. His books include a two-volume study of *Vorticism*, 1976; *Art Beyond the Gallery*, 1985; *David Bomberg*, 1987; *A Bitter Truth: Avant-garde Art and the Great War*, 1994; *Jacob Epstein*, 1999; and *Everything Seemed Possible*, a four-volume collection of his writings on modern art, 2003. He has recently completed *Mercy, Madness, Pestilence and Death*, a history of western art and hospitals from the Renaissance to the twentieth century.

Growing up in the close-packed, boisterous vitality of New York's East Side during the late nineteenth century, Jacob Epstein was fascinated by its multi-racial character. He relished observing and sketching the 'swarms of Russians, Poles, Italians, Greeks and Chinese' who 'lived as much in the streets as in the crowded tenements.'[i] But as a student, western art attracted him most of all. He 'longed to see the originals of Michelangelo and Donatello'[ii], realising that America could provide him with little first-hand experience of the sculpture he valued. Paris did, and after settling there in 1902 he savoured the opportunity provided by the Louvre to become familiar with 'early Greek work, Cyclades Sculpture, the bust known as *The Lady of Elche*, and the limestone bust of Akhenaton.'[iii] He also remembered enjoying 'a mass of primitive sculpture none too well assembled'[iv] at the Trocadero, although it is doubtful whether the work displayed there had any direct effect on Epstein's carvings at this early stage in his career.

The academic instruction he received at the Ecole des Beaux-Arts laid more emphasis on modelling from life and drawing Michelangelo casts. 'In carving there was practically no instruction', he recalled, 'and we were left alone to do pretty well what we pleased.'[v] His subsequent period of study at Julian's also seems to have stressed the importance of working in clay from the model. A visit to Rodin's studio, arranged with the help of Frederick Cayley Robinson, would have confirmed the pre-eminence of modelling when Epstein encountered the prodigious energy of the bronzes on show there. But he also recalled making a 'heroic-sized' sculpture which 'bore a remarkable resemblance' to 'early Egyptian figures',[vi] so even at this early stage Epstein was beginning to look beyond the boundaries of Western inspiration alone.

The first major commission he received after moving to London in 1905 stayed close to Renaissance and Rodinesque sources of inspiration. All eighteen of the over-life-size figures Epstein produced for the facade of the British Medical Association headquarters in the Strand suggest that the influence of classical art was still dominating his imagination.[vii] But his new friendship with Eric Gill soon involved them both in a visionary and collaborative plan for a vast sculptural temple set in six acres of the Sussex countryside. Gill emphasized its ancient, megalithic character by describing it in the autumn of 1910 as 'a great scheme of doing some colossal figures together (as a contribution to the world), a sort of twentieth-century Stonehenge.'[viii] Epstein had previously executed some 'temple' sculpture of his own, although the work has not survived. So he was probably responsible for the initial conception of this ambitious idea, and it must have marked the moment when his work moved beyond Greece, Italy and France to find its stimulus in prehistoric art.

Financial obstacles frustrated the completion of the plan, but one carving that might be linked with this 'Stonehenge' venture is Epstein's *Sun Goddess, Crouching* (1909-10, cat no. 4). It announces his renewed enthusiasm for Egyptian sculpture. And the form of the stone block, announced in the plinth, is retained throughout this remarkable image. We become acutely aware of the block's straightness still obliging her back, sides and front to conform to its cubic identity.

Although modest in size, *Sun Goddess, Crouching* is sufficiently powerful to suggest a figure 'colossal' enough for the temple plan outlined by Gill. It is even more monumental in its implications than the far larger *Sun God*, which can also be related to the Sussex temple project. Epstein continued to deepen the relief of this brazenly naked figure long after he commenced it, but in 1910 the *Sun God* must have been shallow enough to look as if he was growing out of the enormous expanse of Hoptonwood stone. The umbilical link between figure and

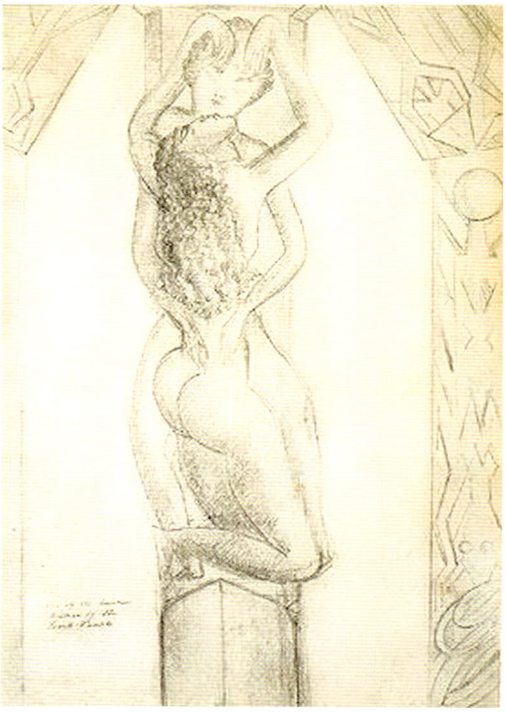

8 Jacob Epstein
One of the Hundred Pillars of the Secret Temple, c.1910

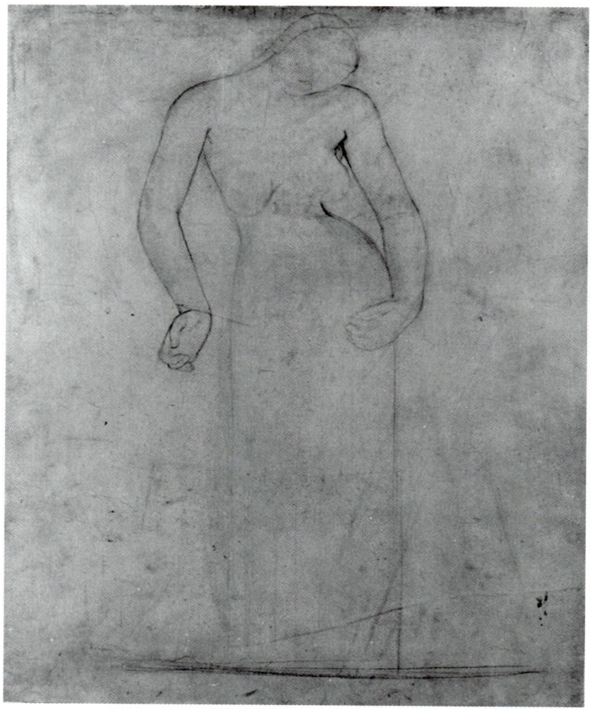

7 Jacob Epstein
Study for Figure of Maternity, c.1910

ground is most spectacularly dramatised in the great mane of Egyptian hair, which flows back from the god's imperious face until its tendrils merge with the stone behind.

Although the 'Stonehenge' venture was abandoned, the surviving work associated with it suggests that this profane temple would have been primarily dedicated to the theme of multi-racial erotic gratification. Epstein's drawing, *One of the Hundred Pillars of the Secret Temple* (c.1910, cat no. 8) is almost as direct in its celebration of sexual pleasure as Gill's extraordinary carving *Ecstasy*, which boldly represents the moment of copulation itself. Both men were determined to emancipate such subjects from the puritanism, hypocrisy and prurience of British society's attitudes towards the delights of the flesh, and their audacity was courageous. But no less innovative was their adherence to the inspiration of heretical cultures lying far outside the approved Hellenic and Renaissance models. Epstein haunted the British Museum, where he found himself becoming particularly excited by 'the Egyptian rooms and the vast and wonderful collections from Polynesia and Africa.'[ix]

When Epstein was photographed with his *Maternity* (*Study for Figure of Maternity*, cat no. 7) in 1910, her hair likewise appeared to be growing out of the roughly-hewn mass of stone. Although he subsequently refined the back of her head until it achieved an unusual degree of smoothness, large expanses of this major carving were left incomplete. But she still amounts to a brazen celebration of fecundity.

Compared with the *Maternity* he completed two years earlier for the British Medical Association building, which calmly adhered to the European tradition, this new carving unequivocally rejects the Western norm. Instead, it embraces alternatives culled from Indian and African sources, and most of the viewers who encountered *Maternity* at the Albert Hall in 1912 were quite unprepared for Epstein's provocative new interpretation of womanhood. They would have been shocked above all by the seemingly wanton flaunting of her sexuality. Although this serene mother lowers her Asian eyes to contemplate the roundness of her stomach, she exudes the intensely physical allure which brought about her impregnation.

Although Gill was scarcely exaggerating when he wrote in his diary that Epstein was 'quite mad about sex',[x] *Maternity* also possesses a considerable amount of tenderness and dignified restraint. So does *The Tomb of Oscar Wilde* (Fig. 8, see also *Study for Tomb of Oscar Wilde, 1909-11*, cat no. 5) by far the largest and most lengthily considered carving Epstein ever produced. He created a 'flying demon-angel'[xi] floating entirely free of the plinth below and emerging instead from the side of a great stone block. Epstein arrived at this ingenious hovering position by applying the same principle that had recently informed his *Sun God* relief. For the angel grows out of his ground in a similarly organic manner, and the streamlined Assyrian sweep of his wings remains wholly faithful to the flank of the stone itself.

When Epstein travelled to Paris, in 1912, for the installation of the Wilde carving in Père Lachaise Cemetery, he made friendships that encouraged him to work in an even more radical manner. Modigliani, like him a Jewish artist far from home, proved especially congenial. Epstein never forgot seeing the 'miserable hole of a studio' where Modigliani had carved 'nine or ten of those long heads which were suggested by African masks.'[xii] They confirmed Epstein in his passion for so-called primitive art, and Brancusi persuaded him that his last vestiges of enthusiasm for Michelangelo must now be jettisoned. Epstein never forgot how Brancusi 'would pluck at the back of his hand and pinch the flesh, "Michelangelo", he would say, "beef steak!"'[xiii]

On his return to England, Epstein's radicalism intensified. Settling in the remoteness of Pett Level on the Sussex coast, he set to work on carvings even more elemental than anything produced earlier in his career. Two images of a pregnant woman were made from flenite, a dark green serpentine stone. The very word 'flenite', Epstein's own nickname, evoked not only the hardness of granite but the prehistoric associations of flint. And both these women inhabit a primeval world as surely as the archaistic mother and baby in another carving called *Flenite Relief*.

The larger of the two women, *Figure in Flenite*, adopts a defensive attitude to the life swelling inside her stomach. She cranes her Polynesian face forwards in an apprehensive way, but the sheer block-like solidity of her dress counteracts at least some of the anxiety she transmits. Epstein honoured the integrity of his flenite material in order to convey sturdy resilience as well as awesome primeval trepidation. And when he revealed the legs of a similar woman in *Female Figure in Flenite*, her limbs turned out to be indomitably stocky. In Paris, Brancusi had counselled Epstein against imitating the 'primitive' carvings they both admired. And *Female Figure in Flenite* avoids that danger by fusing its Polynesian inspiration with a wholly personal response to a woman's body. This mother, for all her prehistoric 'barbarity', is absorbed in a poignant concern for the baby growing in her stomach. One angry critic accused the flenite figures of 'rude savagery, flouting respectable tradition – vague memories of dark ages as distant from modern feeling as the lives of the Martians.'[xiv] But Epstein evokes these 'dark ages' in order to recover atavistic truths about motherhood, birth and sexuality which he thought 'modern feeling'[xv] was in danger of forgetting.

All the figures in his carvings of this period share the same sense of unfathomable 'primitive' strangeness. It is as if Epstein wanted to return to the distant origins of sculpture. In the exquisite marble *Mother and Child*, facial features are minimally defined so that he can explore the full contrast between the baby's convex rotundity and the woman's concave elongation. Around the same time, possibly to emphasize the enigma of existence, the face of Epstein's first marble *Venus* remains impenetrably blank. She keeps her secret, and affirms complete serenity even while maintaining a precarious poise on the sloping back of the dove beneath her feet. This amply built Venus, with her dangling African breasts and heavy buttocks, seems to be encouraging the doves in their copulation below.

Six years and a world war came between the completion of Epstein's *Venus* figures and his next carved sculpture. Even then the outcome was a pair of surprisingly classical *Marble Arms*, so dutiful in their anatomical propriety that they excluded too much of Epstein's individual vision as an artist. Only in *Genesis* (Fig. 6, see also *Genesis II,* cat no. 19), carved in 1929-30, did he fully recover his involvement with non-western cultures. The heavily African treatment of the head reflects his accelerating passion for acquiring 'primitive' carvings.

Epstein's immense collection was especially remarkable for its holdings of West African sculpture. The face in *Genesis* reflects that enthusiasm quite literally, in the hope of conveying what he later described as 'the eternal primeval feminine, the mother of the race.' His overall aim in this uninhibited image was to produce a 'serene and majestic' alternative to all the 'coquetries and fanciful erotic nudes of modern sculpture.'[xvi]

But he achieved a greater unity between head and body in the dramatic *Woman Possessed* two years later. From her bunched fists to her stubby feet, this carving presents a woman transported by an ecstasy which seems organic in implications. It is surely no accident that the great De Mire sale in Paris was held in the same year as the making of *Woman Possessed*. For Epstein acquired, from this outstanding collection on offer at the Hotel Drouot, a standing figure from the Gabon River which he claimed 'equals anything that has come out of Africa.' In his view, this towering wooden man with hallucinatory eyes 'has the astounding attitude of being held spell-bound by sorcery,' [xvii] an observation that applies equally well to *Woman Possessed*. The De Mire figure may even have helped Epstein to construct his taut and disciplined carving, for it contains an extreme of heightened emotion within a body from which every trace of superfluous

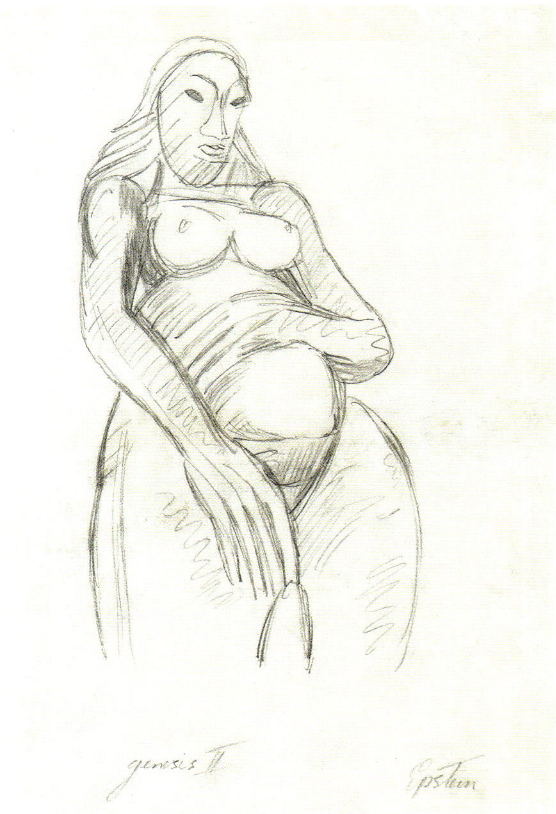

above:
19 Jacob Epstein
Genesis II, 1929-30

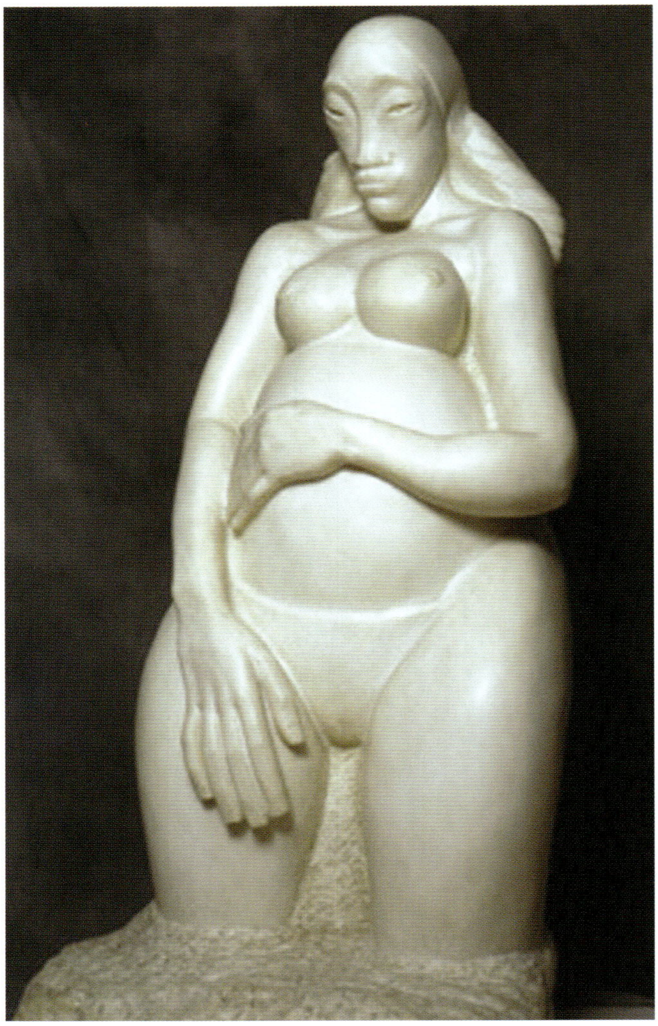

Fig. 6 Jacob Epstein
Genesis, 1929-31 (detail)
Catalogue only

frenzy has been ruthlessly expunged. But it would be unwise to search for close connections between the two images. By this time, Epstein was capable of absorbing African inspiration within his individual form-language, an achievement which becomes still more striking when *Woman Possessed* is compared with the mother in *Flenite Relief* twenty years earlier. Although her body was arrested in a similarly arched position, the little flenite woman was far more 'archaic' in structure than the 1932 carving. Just as Brancusi would have wished, Epstein now succeeded in establishing complete independence while continuing to rely on the African example as a yardstick for his own attempts to arrive at the heart of human experience.

He must have been aware of the consistency of purpose behind works as far apart in date as *Flenite Relief and Woman Possessed*, for both carvings were included in his 1933 one-man show at the Leicester Galleries. There was indeed a striking continuity linking the pre-war carvings with the latest products of his chisel. However much these images earned him the respect of younger sculptors like Henry Moore, who at that time regarded direct carving as the pinnacle of his ambitions, they did not earn Epstein any praise from a wider public. In 1931, the *Daily Express* had denounced *Genesis* as a 'MONGOLIAN MORON THAT IS OBSCENE.'[xviii] Similar hysteria greeted the most powerful of his later carvings also.

Vituperation was duly heaped on *Behold the Man*, Epstein's colossus of the mid-1930s. His choice of the *Ecce Homo* subject showed how far he had wandered from the orthodox Jewish beliefs espoused by his family. But he was still deeply interested in religious feeling and, as Anthony Blunt remarked when the unfinished stone was first exhibited in 1935, Epstein's interest in 'primitive' carvings sprang from a belief that their makers had 'offered a new way of making statements about the super-natural. True, the religious and superstitious ideas which they sought to express were remote from those of Christianity, but they both existed on the same supernatural plane, and it would be worth trying whether their methods could not be adapted to the needs of European art.'[xix]

An amalgam of 'primitive' and Renaissance styles does indeed account for *Behold the Man*'s overbearing power. If the carving appears simplified to the point of crudeness, it does at least remain faithful to the massive stone which prompted Epstein to expend so much energy on its creation. It is as totemic, in its way, as the tall marble Venuses, even if the coolness of the latter statues was now replaced by a more turbulent mood. *Behold the Man* is a particularly autobiographical work, evincing the sculptor's determination to continue carving in the face of the most dispiriting antagonism. In this respect, it seems appropriate that the statue remained in Epstein's studio until his death – even though, as Blunt pointed out, it deserved 'to be placed in a church, where it would be seen from a distance and would make its appeal instantly.'[xx]

Epstein returned to his old fascination with Egyptian art when he carved the large block of alabaster which became known as *Consummatum Est*. Although this predominantly Egyptian figure sports an Assyrian beard, Epstein was also affected by the medieval alabaster tradition of his adopted country. The title *It Is Finished* is redolent of death's finality; and yet Epstein, with typical stubbornness, refuses to produce a quiescent image of extinction. The patriarch's outstretched hands have the vigour of life about them, and the head seems to be raised up in defiance of mortality. Despite Epstein's melancholy realisation that no one wanted such a deeply pondered work, that 'it came from me and returns to me in a world where it is not wanted', [xxi] he refused to be defeated by the ignominy of neglect.

On the contrary, just over a year after he finished this magisterial memorial to the departed, the irrepressible carver set to work on a titantic celebration of 'primitive' man at his most alive and potent. This dynamism is the most conspicuous quality of a carving that surges upwards, gathering power as it moves in an expansive momentum towards the arching pectorals and aspirant head above. Without indulging in any outflung gestures, which would have impaired the figure's compressed energy and flouted the integrity of the original block, Epstein infuses *Adam* with a truly primordial vitality.

In many ways it summarizes everything he had learned from non-western sculpture. Earthbound and yet determined to push as far towards the sky as possible, *Adam* represents the most restless and indeed reckless side of Epstein's temperament. No wonder he admitted that 'into no other work had I merged myself so much.'[xxii]

He made this confessional remark before going on to execute the most turbulent, complex and personal carving of his later years. If Epstein identified himself with *Adam*, he seems to have projected himself even more ardently into the human protagonist who strives against divine opposition in *Jacob and the Angel*. The two Jacobs shared the same name, after all, and throughout his life Epstein had regarded carving essentially as a prolonged struggle with the massive blocks of matter he liked best. The alabaster employed for *Jacob and the Angel* was one of the most enormous he had ever handled, and the effort he expended on its shaping was as prodigious, in its way, as the long nocturnal wrestling match which Jacob undertook with the winged figure. Moreover, the structure of the carving reinforces the idea that Jacob is battling, not only with a divine agent but also with the megalithic slab of stone itself.

Even so, *Jacob and the Angel* marks the last occasion when Epstein infused a major carving with the 'primitive' intensity he had once valued so highly. From now on, non-western influences began to fade in his work, and the post-war stone figure of *Lazarus* marks a return to his youthful sources of stimulus. Memories of Michelangelo's *Captives* had once more surfaced in Epstein's mind, forty years after they first helped to inspire some of his British Medical Association figures. But compared with Michelangelo's straining, muscular prisoners, *Lazarus* seems barely able to sustain the life which has so miraculously returned to him. Even though frailty cannot be found in most of Epstein's carved work, the ageing sculptor's awareness of mortality allowed him to give this elegiac statue a quite new apprehension of the ultimate vulnerability of man.

[i] Jacob Epstein *Let There Be Sculpture: The Autobiography of Jacob Epstein* (London: Michael Joseph, 1940), p.1
[ii] Ibid., p.22
[iii] Ibid., p.23
[iv] Ibid
[v] Ibid., p.221
[vi] Epstein refers to it as 'a group of "sunworshippers"', but some images published in *The World*, 27 Oct 1912 prove that these figures (now lost) were Rodinesque in inspiration
[vii] For a full account of the BMA statues in the Strand, see Richard Cork, *Art Beyond the Gallery in Early 20th-Century England* (New Haven and London: Yale University Press, 1985), Chapter One
[viii] Eric Gill to William Rothenstein, 25 September 1910, ed. Walter Shewring *Letters of Eric Gill* (London: Jonathan Cape, 1947), p.32
[ix] Epstein, op. cit., p.32
[x] Eric Gill Diaries, 9 December 1913, Clark Library, Los Angeles
[xi] Epstein, op. cit., p.51
[xii] Ibid., p.47
[xiii] Ibid., p.64
[xiv] Quoted by T E Hulme, *The New Age*, 25 December 1913
[xv] Ibid
[xvi] Epstein, op. cit., p.162
[xvii] Ibid., p.217
[xviii] *Daily Express*, 7 February 1931
[xix] Anthony Blunt, *The Spectator*, 15 March 1935
[xx] Ibid.
[xxi] Epstein, op. cit., p. 178.
[xxii] Ibid., p.195.

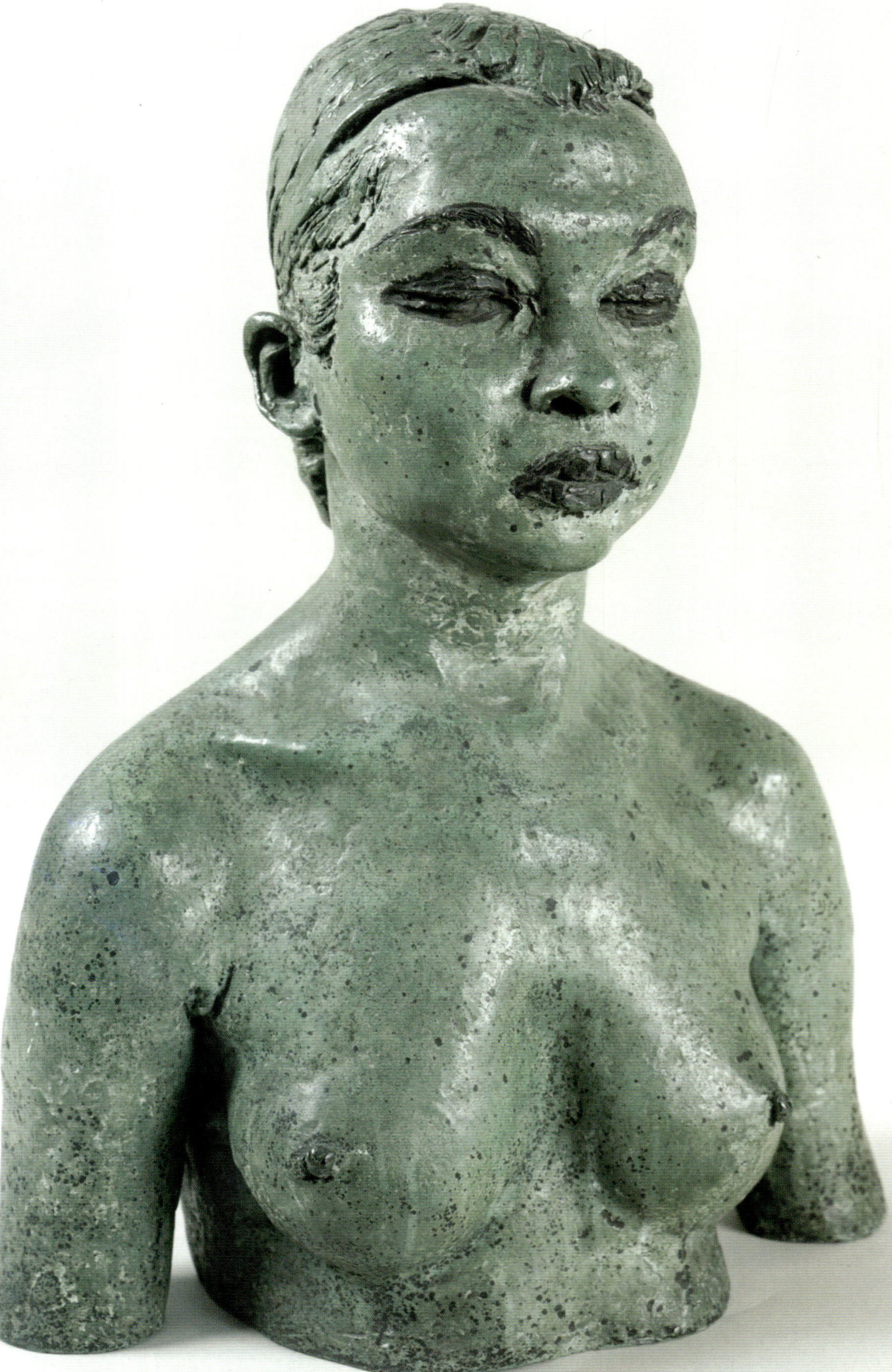

24 Jacob Epstein
Rani Rama, 1934

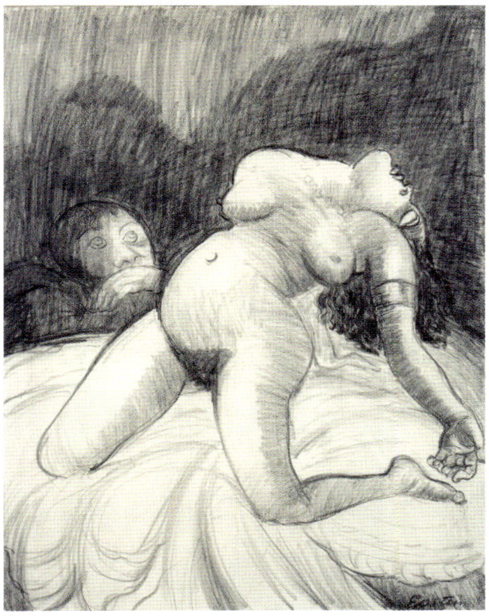

26 Jacob Epstein
Illustration for Les Fleurs du Mal, 1938

Epstein the Enigma

Victor Arwas

Victor Arwas is an acknowledged authority on the fine and decorative arts of the late nineteenth and twentieth centuries. He is the author of many books on Art Nouveau, the Russian Avant Garde and the Arts and Crafts Movement, artists' monographs, museum catalogues and articles; he has organised and curated exhibitions in Britain, the United States, Japan and The Netherlands, lectures and broadcasts widely. As a collector and director of the Victor Arwas Gallery, London, he has participated in many international museum exhibitions organised by the Victoria & Albert Museum, Tate Gallery, Barbican Gallery, and the Ben Uri Gallery in London; the Kunsthal, Rotterdam; Van Gogh, Amsterdam; Seita, Paris; Caixa. Barcelona; Quebec, Canada; the Jewish Museum in New York, and the Jerusalem and Tel Aviv Museums. He is preparing major books on Art Deco and Modernism.

In his very first interview with Arnold Haskell for *The Sculptor Speaks*, published in 1931, Jacob Epstein cut the ground under the feet of any writer attempting to make sense of the artist's work: "don't make the mistake of thinking that a work of art can be explained."[i] And again, "No one can explain a work of art," adding as the *coup de grâce* "least of all the artist."[ii] In the sixth interview he returned to the subject: "I certainly will not explain my work. The explanation lies in the work itself. It is my last word."[iii] Haskell described him as "a man of superior intelligence and culture, with a more than ordinary knowledge of music and literature... [who] possesses an extremely balanced and logical mind."[iv] This helped him survive and surmount such waves of vilification, vituperation, and sheer hatred that few other artists have had to endure.

Much of this was caused by a parochial distrust of all things perceived as 'foreign': Epstein was American born, a Jew, cosmopolitan in outlook, avant-garde in conception, combative under critical fire, indomitable in his vision. He was clearly a threat to the comfortable vision an English gentleman had of his world. For although these attacks were orchestrated by newspapers (and not merely the downmarket popular ones), many of the most vociferous attackers were respected, respectable writers, painters, sculptors, politicians and religious leaders.

It is a paradox that the more Epstein was attacked, the greater was his fame. The great public, with not the slightest interest in any form of art, was nevertheless fascinated by the man who created such 'atrocities' and flocked to view them at the seaside freak show 'Chamber of Horrors' in Liverpool set up by the Tussaud Wax Museum, or lined up ready to pay their pennies to go through the turnstile at the Leicester Galleries' exhibitions of his work. However vilified, the name of Epstein was more familiar than that of any other living artist.

In the process, Epstein also attracted many supporters, including a number of artists, some of whom became friends and some even remained friends, though several who supported him publicly did not always understand or appreciate individual work, and often said so. Others were ambiguous in their praise. Henry Moore, helped, praised and encouraged by Epstein, disliked much of his work, referred to him as "scarcely an innovator let alone a revolutionary"[v] and occasionally opposed the public siting of some of it, although in his *Times* obituary he generously acknowledged his own and other artists' debt to Epstein: "He took the brickbats, he took the insults, he faced the howls of derision...And as far as sculpture in this century is concerned he took them first."[vi]

Although not a practising Jew, Epstein was steeped in Jewish lore and tradition, and absorbed its humanity and humanistic outlook. He kept a *Menorah*, the seven-branched candlestick, prominently displayed on a sideboard, and always retained his *taleth,* the prayer shawl that later doubles as a shroud. He frequently read his Bible, and in 1932 exhibited fifty-four large pencil and watercolour drawings illustrating the Old Testament at the Redfern Gallery (cat no. 21). His was an obsessive pursuit of a subject, gnawing at it persistently, seeking minute variations which allowed him to penetrate deeper into the subject's mysteries, at times visible only to his own very personal vision. Thus he similarly executed hundreds of watercolours of Epping Forest and of flowers, the latter being dispersed in some very successful exhibitions.

In 1936 Epstein met George Macy in Paris. Macy was the founder of the Limited Editions Club in New York, which commissioned illustrated editions of works from many distinguished artists, and these were issued to subscribers, though several were later reprinted in cheaper editions sold to the public. One of its odder publications was James Joyce's *Ulysses:* Matisse was commissioned to execute the illustrations, but never having read or even heard of Joyce, delivered illustrations derived from Homer. Invited to choose a book to illustrate, Epstein chose Baudelaire's *Les Fleurs du Mal* and undertook to produce between fifteen and twenty drawings (cat no. 26, *Illustration for Fleurs du Mal*). He had read and admired the poems over the years, and steeped himself in their symbolism. Two years later, Epstein produced sixty powerful, intense, harshly erotic drawings which he considered to be among his finest. Thirty-seven of them were exhibited at the Tooth Gallery in New Bond Street.

Epstein's studies at the Ecole des Beaux-Arts in Paris enabled him to study models and plaster replicas of masterly sculptures, and experiment with modelling clay. He regularly destroyed everything he modelled, absorbing the living language of clay, its ability to alternately absorb and reflect light. Though useful, this did not entirely satisfy him, as there was no instruction in carving, and he spent less time at the Beaux-Arts to study at the Académie Julian and later at the Académie Colarossi. Much of his time was spent in the Louvre Museum, studying Greek, Roman, Egyptian, Assyrian and other sculpture. He haunted all other available museums, studying the great works of the Renaissance and the primitive works in the Musée de l'Homme. When he came to London, he continued his exposure to all the extraordinary ways man has explained his existence and his relationship to the great unknown, primarily in sculpture, in every civilisation, every epoch, every country. The British Museum, the South Kensington Museum, the National Gallery, all expanded his visual horizons, as did his equally expanding collection of African, Oceanic, pre-Columbian, Egyptian and other artefacts. Largely disregarded as 'primitive' trinkets and tourist souvenirs, they appealed to Epstein's realisation that many of these objects had sacramental, ceremonial or magical properties, and were the embodiment of various systems of belief and worship. His collection, each piece carefully and intuitively chosen, eventually became one of the most important such collections in private hands. It was, unfortunately, dispersed after his death. (Fig. 7 *Sandstone Figure of a Hindu Goddess*).

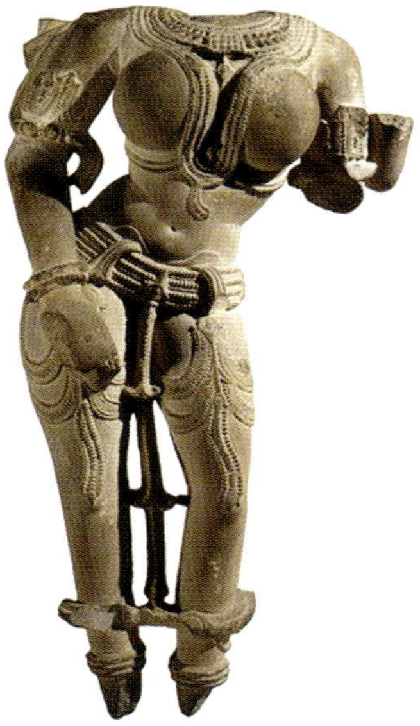

Fig. 7 ***Sandstone Figure of a Hindu Goddess,***
Possibly from Rajasthan, India, 11th century AD
Formerly owned by Sir Jacob Epstein
The British Museum, London

His recognition of the numinous in so many varied forms, combined with a passionate desire to create major monuments, led to the creation of many Christian subjects, though he realised how much he would be attacked for this. After showing his first bronze sculpture of *Christ* in 1920, the reaction of a somewhat racially confused Father Bernard Vaughan in *The Graphic* included the memorable words: "I have stood in front and at the back elevation of this gross and grotesque thing, with nose turned up and feet turned in; I have stood on the right and the left of this offending and hurting caricature; I have studied the unshapely head, the receding brow, the thick lips, the untipped nose, the uncanny eyes, the poorly built body, with its ugly feet and uglier hands, till I felt ready to cry out with indignation that in this Christian England there should be exhibited the figure of a Christ which suggested to me some degraded Chaldean or African, which wore the appearance of an Asiatic-American or Hun-Jew, which reminded me of some emaciated Hindu, or a badly grown Egyptian swathed in the cerements of the grave."[vii]

Undeterred by this, Epstein continued to depict figures of Christ and the Virgin Mary until in his seventies, time and the changing times convincing both the Church of England and the Roman Catholic Church that he was, indeed, a supreme interpreter of their most profound beliefs. Driving himself relentlessly, he produced a huge, impressive *Christ in Majesty* for the rebuilt Llandaff Cathedral, a huge bronze of *St. Michael and the Devil* for the new Coventry Cathedral and, what is undoubtedly one of the most beautiful statues in London, the *Madonna and Child* on the central front wall of the Convent of the Holy Child in Cavendish Square.

Epstein was a master of both modelling and carving. Few sculptors actually carve. To be face to face with, say, a five-ton block of marble, granite, or other stone must be a daunting prospect. As often as not the block was placed high on the façade of a building, and he had to climb up ladders, perch on scaffolding and brave the often inclement weather. Epstein frequently worked with twenty-ton blocks. Some were so hard that many of his chisels and points broke without penetrating the stone. He had to seek makers of appropriate tools and exert great strength as well as great delicacy in freeing his creation from the heart of the stone. Most sculptors made a clay or wax model which was then carved by professional stone-masons and architectural carvers, using stone-cutting machinery for the bulk of the work to whatever size the artist required. Even Rodin did this.

The desire to carve great monuments tantalised and tormented Epstein. He and Eric Gill became good friends. Both were hungrily sexual, though Gill was more omnivorous. Gill was a master of lettering, and carved the titles of a couple of Epstein's sculptures (see cat no. 6). Together they devised a scheme of building a great temple in the countryside, a modern Stonehenge in which huge sculptures would be placed, but lack of funds killed the scheme. Gill blamed Epstein's lack of enthusiasm, and became a hostile critic. In fact, it seems unlikely that Gill would ever have carried out the scheme. He was a superb wood-engraver and etcher, and confined much of his sculpture to small religious or erotic subjects. When Count Harry Kessler, the publisher, sent him to Paris with an introduction to Maillol, Gill arrived there, walked a little in the streets, did not have the courage to see Maillo and came straight back to England.

Epstein's first major commission in 1908 was a series of egihteen statues, greater than life-size, for the façade of the new British Medical Association building in the Strand. They represented Primal Energy, Matter, Hygeia Goddess of Medicine and Health, Chemical Research, Academic Research, Mentality, Youth, an old woman presenting a new-born baby, Man, Maternity and some Dancing Figures. Though discreetly located high up the building, they unleashed a storm of protests, largely because of their nudity. Many artists and others rallied to his cause, and the statues were finally allowed to stay. In 1935 the building was sold to the Government of Southern Rhodesia, which announced the statues were to be removed. Return of the storm. Once again the statues were reprieved, but only for two years. In 1937 bunting was suspended from some of the statues for the coronation of King George VI. Its removal caused a small piece of stone to break off. This was used as the 'public safety' excuse to mutilate the statues by smashing large parts of all of them.

In 1910 Epstein was commissioned to design a tomb for Oscar Wilde in the Père Lachaise cemetery in Paris. Inspired by Wilde's poem *The Sphinx*, Epstein carved a powerful winged figure from a twenty-ton block of Hoptonwood stone. Scandal pursued the artist. The cemetery authorities considered the sculpture obscene because the figure was equipped with genitalia. Covered with a tarpaulin, and guarded by a gendarme. the figure then had its genitals covered in plaster. Epstein removed the plaster and the tarpaulin came on again. Wilde's friend and executor Robert Ross finally equipped the figure with a large bronze fig leaf, and the statue was eventually unveiled in 1914. Some years later the bronze fig leaf was stolen and presented to Epstein by Aleister Crowley (known to his followers as 'The Great Beast') in London. After a long and tranquil period of slow natural aging as the focus of both literary and amorous visitors of various interests, the flying demon-angel re-entered public notoriety when a person or persons unknown mutilated it in 1961 by hacking off its testicles, apparently the action of two English ladies.[viii] The tomb is a site of pilgrimage for lovers. Much of it is covered with lipstick kisses.

Epstein could never resist the appeal of a huge, virginal block of stone. He rarely attacked it with a wholly predetermined plan. Unconstrained by the demands of a commission, he could please himself by pursuing his inner vision and marrying it with the demands, parameters, qualities and limitations of the material under his hands. He strove to achieve a monumental effect, his subjects the essence of his own entirely human, humane, humanistic beliefs, a pantheism filtered through the verbal and visual imagery of the Bible. His carved creations were often the butt of the startled jokes of the uncomprehending masses and many of the equally uncomprehending arbiters of taste. Curiously enough, it has taken the triumph of abstract art over a period of years for his creations to lose their initial shock appearance and become almost cosily familiar, so that the strength and power of these Epstein elementals also reveal the tenderness within them.

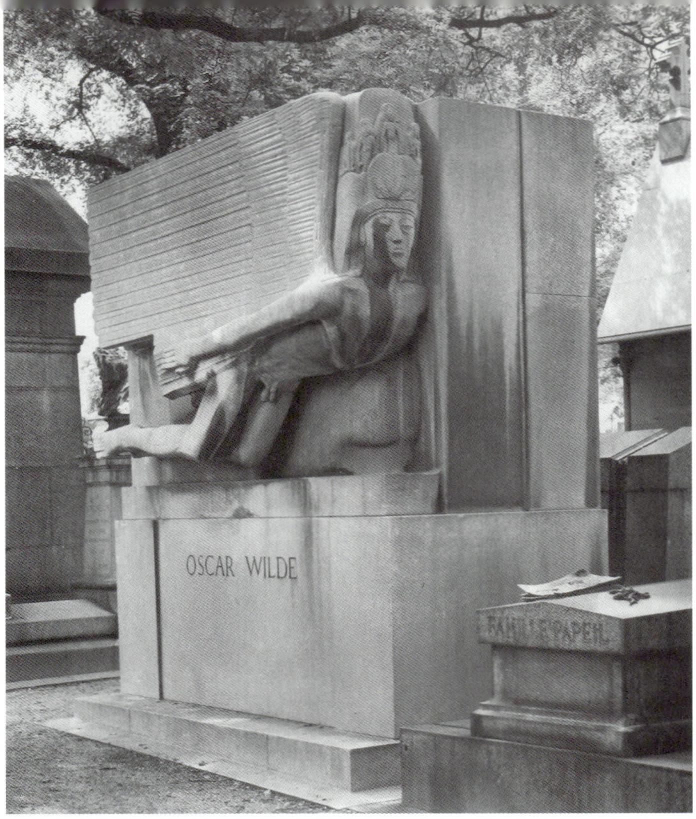

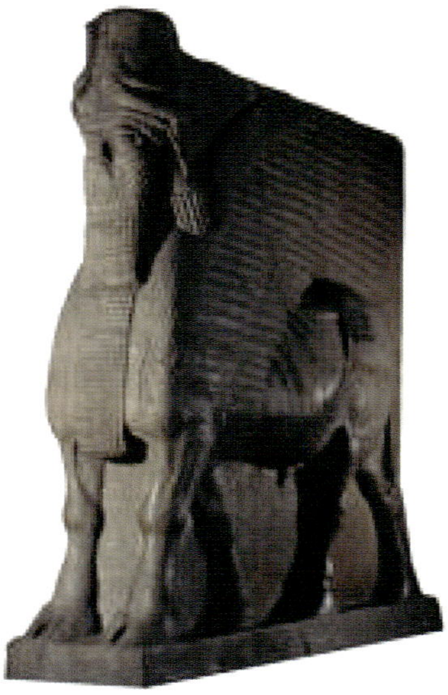

Fig. 8 Jacob Epstein
The Tomb of Oscar Wilde, Paris. 1909-12

Fig. 9 *Colossal Winged Bull from the Palace of Sargon II*,
Khorsabad, Northern Iraq
Neo-Assyrian, c.710-705 BC

5 Jacob Epstein
Study for Tomb of Oscar Wilde, 1909-11

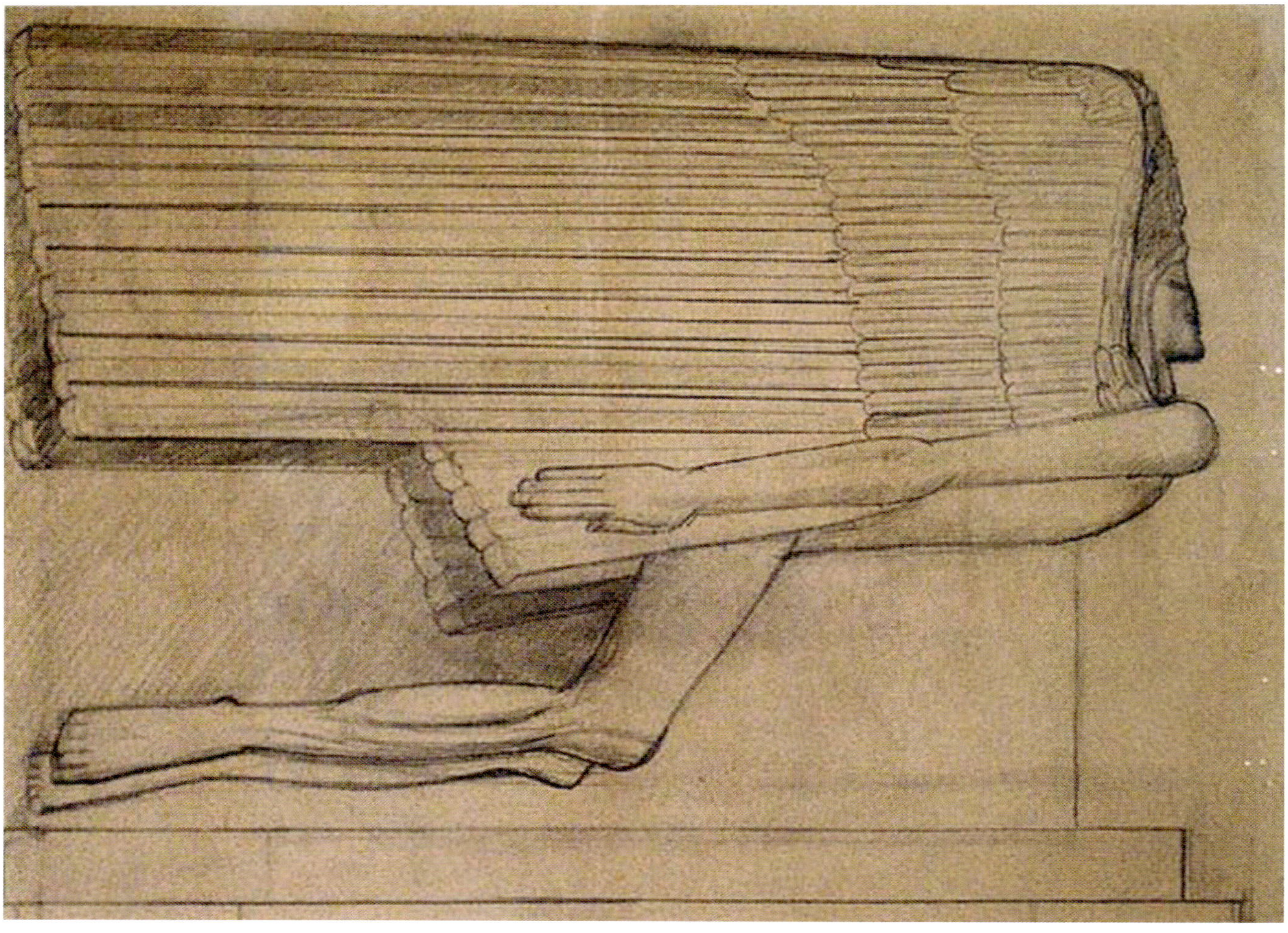

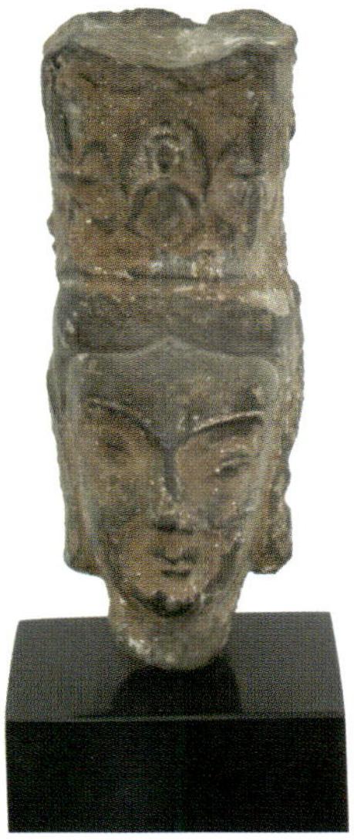

49 *Head of a Bodhisattva,*
c.6-7th century

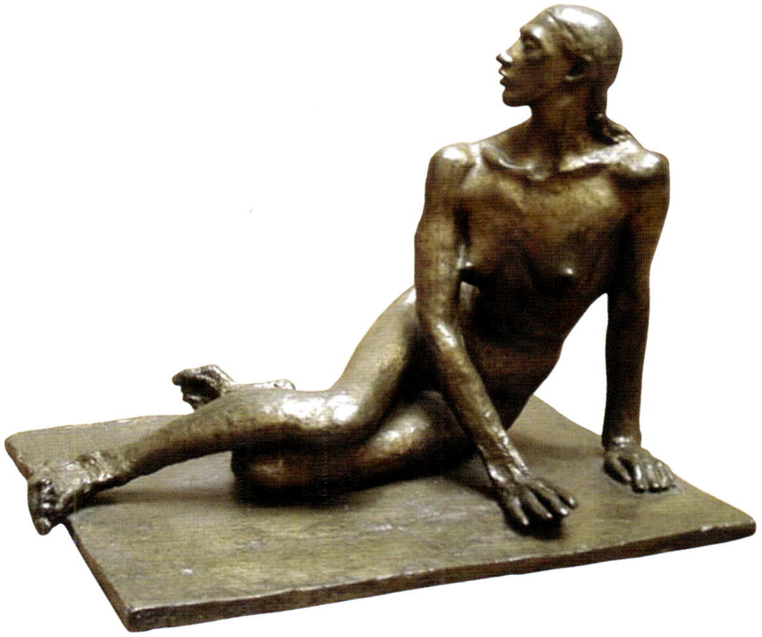

9 Jacob Epstein
Nan the Dreamer, 1911

Having survived their apprenticeship in the prisons of derision they have at last entered appropriate and sympathetic settings.

Admirers of Epstein's carvings often tend to denigrate his portrait heads and busts as mere commercial endeavours. Admirers of his portrait heads and busts often tend to denigrate his carvings as not quite successful. In fact, he never discriminated between the two: carving and modelling were just two sides of the same artistic coin. While he sometimes grumbled at having to accept so many portrait commissions to earn his living, it never prevented him from pursuing those he wished to portray. In the end his body of portraits is a formidable array of famous persons and an equally formidable array of otherwise anonymous faces which have become familiar because he chose them.

Famous sitters tend to end up in museums and other institutions, which is understandable. Joseph Conrad, Albert Einstein, T S Eliot, Emperor Haile Selassie, W Somerset Maugham, Pandit Nehru, George Bernard Shaw, Chaim Weizmann, Yehudi Menuhin, Rabindranath Tagore; statesmen, politicians, actors, musicians, writers, military men, are at the forefront of institutional wish-lists. Perhaps the most popular head is that of Winston Churchill, yet it was used as the focus of a bizarre attack on the reputation of the artist twelve years after his death. On 21 February 1971, *The Sunday Times* published an article claiming that, although it was accepted that the Churchill head was cast in an edition of ten, "*Sunday Times* correspondents throughout the world able to trace no fewer than twelve Epstein busts of Churchill in public and private collections [sic]."[ix] These correspondents were clearly not as diligent as they might have been: after all, Evelyn Silber in her magnificent Catalogue Raisonné of *The Sculpture of Epstein* lists twenty-seven casts. The article goes off into the realm of fantasy, claiming that: "Most sculptors, when they produce an edition, number each cast. The third cast of, say, an edition of six would be franked 3/6. It is also conventional procedure for the caster to break the original mould after the edition is complete." The habit of numbering an edition occurs when an edition is announced, usually by a commercial gallery. Because of the cost of casting, chasing and polishing a bronze, a full edition is rarely cast unless there are guaranteed immediate sales, so the moulds are retained and casts taken as and when required. Thus the numbering of an edition may only mean that it is the maximum number they wish to issue. This historically hardly ever applies to works that collectors actually want. The English 'New Sculptors' cast as many or as few of their works as they could sell. Low numbers were more the result of high price or lack of demand. In France, where legislation regulates most aspects of the art market, casts of nineteenth-century bronzes were frequently between forty and a hundred, depending on popularity. It was only in 1968 that numbering and dating of casts and mention of copyright became mandatory. The Rodin Museum still periodically recasts a number of bronzes to feed the needs of institutions and collectors. The following Sunday the paper returned to the subject, and printed a letter from a woman who wrote that she had cherished her bust of Churchill until reading the article, after which she was so disgusted she hurled it down the cellar steps. Unfortunately the paper did not reveal the address of the cellar.

Epstein was temperamentally incapable of turning out a perfunctory head. He studied each one in detail, looking at each feature in different lights, his concentration totally focused. Each is a psychological *tour de force*, the outcome of what he sees in the features, not what he knows of the sitter's personality; the few that fail do so because he tries too hard to extract a personality that may not warrant such close inspection. He never worried about getting a likeness or flattering his sitter. The likeness appeared in the lumps of clay in his fingers, and the faces came vividly to life, each plane lovingly honed and caressed into expressive personality. "The face is made up of numberless small planes and it is a study of where those planes begin and end, their direction, that makes the individual head."[x]

This is particularly successful in his treatment of women's faces: Nan Condron, a Gypsy girl who attached herself to his household, gaunt and wearily graceful (*Nan the Dreamer,* 1911, cat no. 10); Euphemia Lamb, a shy, dreamy English rose; Meum Lindsell-Stewart (a very pretty young girl who was for a while one of Mr. Cochran's Young Ladies, and posed nude for Gerald Brockhurst, had an affair with Epstein and bore him a child) was clearly a fascinating creature he visualised in different moods – a bronze of a sophisticated flapper with a fan and, in complete contrast, presented in the Mask (cat no. 14 *Third Portrait of Meum (Mask)*) as a hieratic idol, with the pyramidal hair of an Indian Temple carving, the closed eyes and slightly parted lips an echo of his drawing of her in mid-orgasm; the extraordinary Marchesa Casati, who had a pet panther and a pet python, "with her over-large blood-veined eyes, sat with a basilisk stare…In art, of course, her taste was also for the perverse, and she was enamoured of a mask I had done of Meum and coveted it, but was determined to have it in some odd material, glass lit up, from within."[xi]

It is tempting, and easy to detect elements of African or Eastern art, of Egyptian or Assyrian myths, as much in the portraits as in some of the carvings, though this is an unsatisfying exercise. Epstein absorbed all the multifarious influences, Eastern and primitive and Western and sophisticated, and was able to regurgitate them transformed into his own 'basilisk stare'. He experimented with patinations of various colours: brown, black, golden or green; sculpted a series of nudes, children, new-born babes, each inspiring the next, though he only once created a mechanistic man whose smooth, abstract features somehow threatened his humanity: the *Rock Drill* (cat no. 13, *Study for the Rock Drill*).

He was always attracted to women with strong features: the Indian sisters Sunita and Anita, black women, exotic dancers, great untraditional beauties, such as the tragic Sphinx, Gladys Deacon, later Duchess of Marlborough, later still victim of unnecessary plastic surgery which went wrong, or *La Belle Juive* (Betty Joel), or *Rani Rama* (cat no. 24) whose lips alone could turn strong men weak. His chief complaint about his male sitters was that by the time they were prominent enough to sit for him they were already old men. As J B Priestley said to him: "It's this way, Epstein. I look upon this bust as an insurance for both of us against getting forgotten. If you get forgotten, there is your bust of *me*. If I am forgotten there is *your* bust of me."[xii]

The overwhelming feeling that emanates from much of Epstein's work is stillness. Time, emotion, activity, is brought to a halt, and each statue is suspended for eternity. Late in life he felt the need to express movement. His over-life-size full-length study of Field Marshal Smuts in Parliament Square sets off jauntily, perched somewhat awkwardly on its plinth. But his final large group, *The Bowater House Group*, is a fascinating exercise in speed and movement. A father, mother, child and dog race into Hyde Park, the dog straining forward while excitedly looking back to make sure the family is still there. Placed high on a plinth, which is an island in the midst of traffic, it has a wonderfully young, somewhat Pagan feel, an enthusiasm fuelled by the accompanying figure of Pan and the yearning of the mother figure, her elongated body prolonged by unnaturally long arms reaching for the unreachable.

Laurie Lee described Epstein thus: "In this face, whose restless eyes conceal nothing, the eyes dominate all else. They are eyes which have seen, seized and projected half-a-century of achievement as rich and original as that of any artist of present times." [xiii]

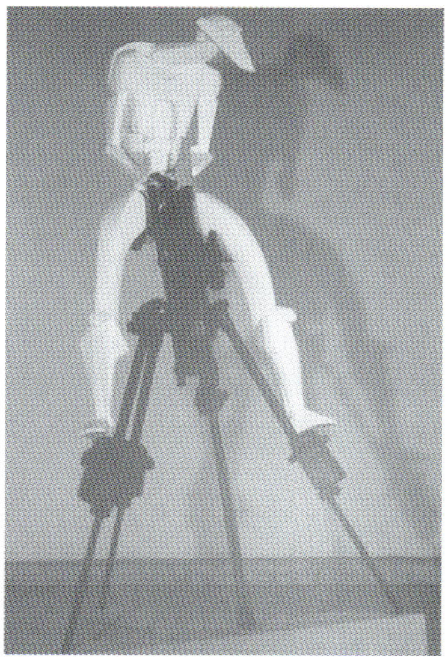

Fig. 10 *Rock Drill: reconstruction*, 1973-4, after the lost original, 1913-15
Catalogue only

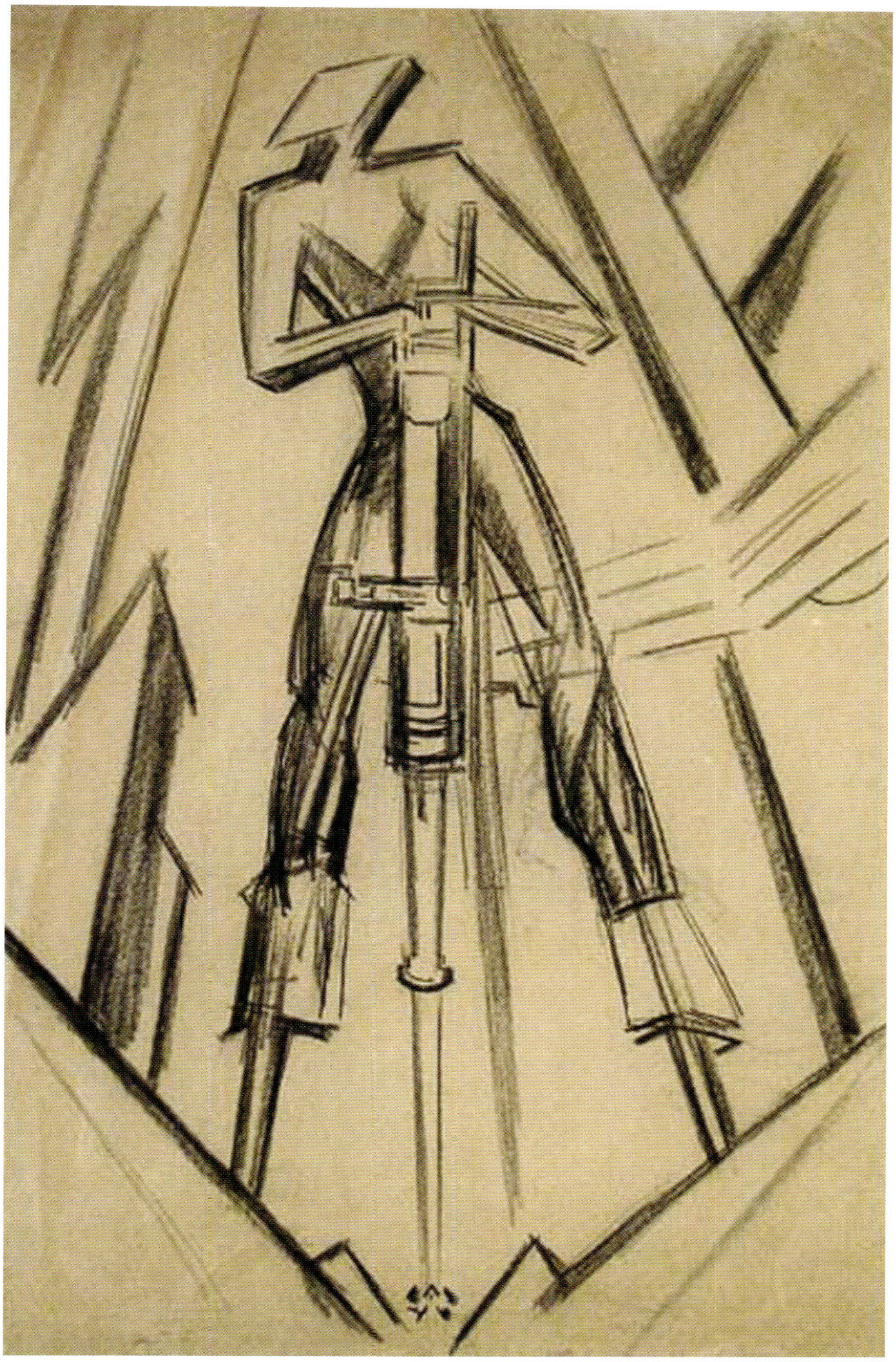

13 Jacob Epstein
Study for the Rock Drill, c.1913

[i] Jacob Epstein to Arnold Haskell *The Sculptor Speaks* (London: William Heinemann, 1931), p. 4
[ii] Ibid., p. IX
[iii] Ibid., p. 64
[iv] Ibid., p. XI
[v] Henry Moore, cited in June Rose *Daemons and Angels* (London: Constable, 2002), p. 185
[vi] Ibid., *The Sunday Times*, 23 August 1959, cited ibid., p. 274
[vii] Jacob Epstein *Let There Be Sculpture: The Autobiography of Jacob Epstein* (London: Michael Joseph, 1940), p.124
[viii] Michael Pennington *An Angel For a Martyr* (Reading: Whiteknights Press, 1987), p. 61
[ix] *The Sunday Times*, 21 February 1971, p. 5
[x] *The Sculptor Speaks*, op. cit., p.78
[xi] Jacob Epstein, *Let There Be Sculpture*, op. cit., pp. 105-6
[xii] Ibid., p.103
[xiii] Geoffrey Ireland/ Laurie Lee, *Epstein* (London: Andre Deutsch & Royal College of Art, not dated), unpaginated

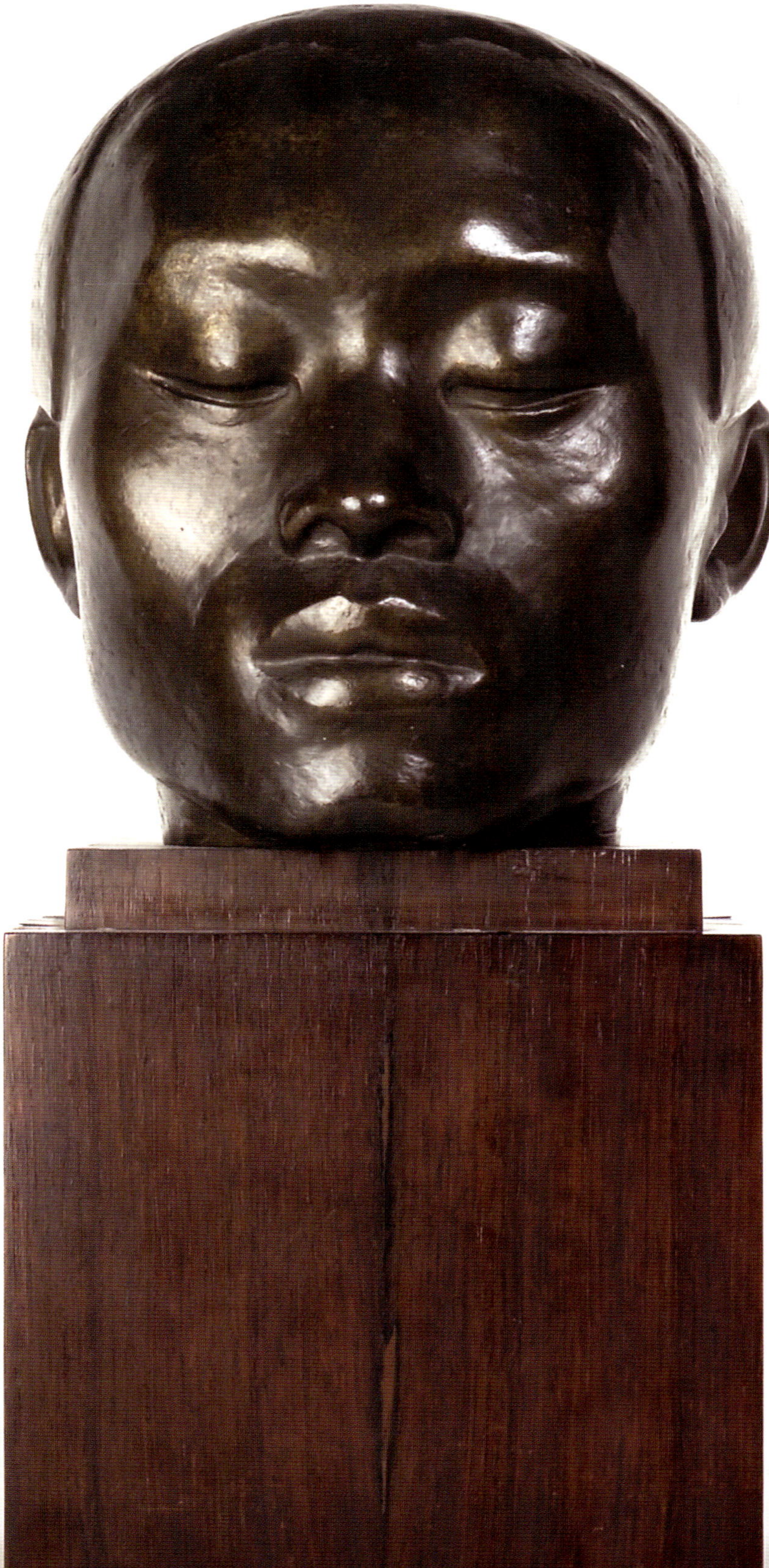

29 Dora Gordine
Chinese Head / Chinaman / Chinese Philosopher, 1926

A Genius for the Exotic

Dora Gordine, Imperialism and the Racial Type in Portraiture

Dr Jonathan Black

AHRB Research Fellow, Dorich House, Kingston University

Dr Jonathan Black obtained his PhD in History of Art (British Art and WWI) from University College London in 2003. He is a specialist in early Twentieth Century Western European art and is the author of: *The Graphic Art of Eric Kennington* (UCL Press, 2001); *The Sculpture of Eric Kennington* (Lund Humphries, 2002) and *Form, Feeling and Calculation: The Paintings and Drawings of Edward Wadsworth* (Philip Wilson, 2005) In 2004 he curated *Blasting the Future: Vorticism in Britain 1910-1920* for the Estorick Collection of Modern Italian Art, London and the Whitworth Art Gallery, University of Manchester, and contributed an essay to the catalogue (Philip Wilson, 2004). He is presently an AHRB Research Fellow in History of Art at Dorich House Museum, Kingston University, researching the life and sculpture of Dora Gordine.

In 1927 a photograph of Gordine's striking *Head of a Chinaman* (also known as *Chinese Head/Chinaman/TheChinese Philosopher*, 1926, cat no. 29) appeared in the French arts magazine *Le Crapouillot* accompanying an article by Lucien Farnoux-Reynaud in which he briskly refuted the alarmist 'yellow peril' arguments advanced by Henri Massis in his recent book *The Defence of the West*.[i] Massis had evidently been heavily influenced by the deep cultural pessimism of Oswald Spengler's seminal *The Decline of the West* (1918-1919) in which he prophesied that Western Civilisation was intrinsically corrupt and doomed to be overwhelmed by the more 'primitive' and yet more vital and uninhibited races of central Asia. The Chinese art critic[ii] sculpted by Gordine does not appear to pose any imminent threat to Western values. If anything, he offers the western European brutalised by the First World War and by fear of Fascism and Bolshevism, a model of civilised restraint and high-minded detachment. In fact Gordine's serene sitter can be located within a debate propelled by André Malraux with the publication in April 1926 of his influential essay *La Tentation de l'Occident* in which he discussed the significance of the hybrid figure of the westernised oriental. Malraux and Farnoux-Reynaud were far more sanguine as to the positive potential of the western mind impacting upon China and how Chinese visiting Paris will make French men see their world with new eyes.[iii]

The first article on Gordine in English, by the notable critic Gerald Reitlinger and published in February

28 Dora Gordine
Guadeloupe Head / Negress, 1928

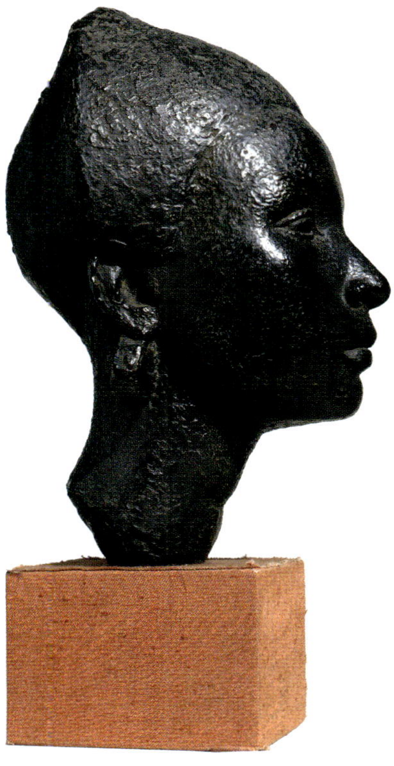

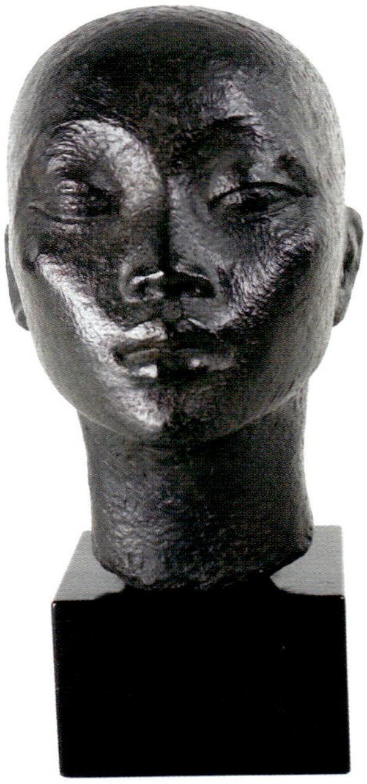

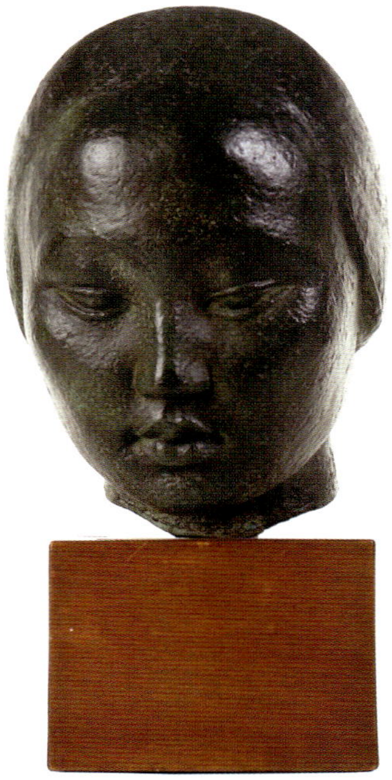

1928, focused on two of her works that he identified as especially 'exotic': *Male Torso* (also known as *Walking Male Torso*) and *Javanese Dancer* (cat no. 30). Gordine was described as: '...a very young Russian sculptor who will shortly come to prominence. At first sight they appear to be very much in the modern Western sculptural tradition which has produced [Charles] Despiau and [Aristide] Maillol and indeed it is to Western academies that their technical tradition is to be attributed. If we regard them a little less superficially it will be found that there is a very un-European spirit behind them. In most statues of dancers we are accustomed to see either a portrait of the dancer, or a symbolic representation of the dance ... in this figure [*Javanese Dancer*] we see the dancer portrayed as a separate species, a human being evolved for the purpose of the dance, a proportion and development determined by the movements of dancing. It is not surprising that a Russian midway between Europe and the East in spirit should have seized it. In the *torso* of the young Cossack rider, every phase of nomad horsemanship seems to be expressed. When some of her exuberant realism has been restrained, a great deal may be expected from this young sculptor.'[iv]

Later that year, responding to Gordine's exhibition in October at the Leicester Galleries, R H Wilenski went so far as to describe 'Miss Gordine' as 'a genius' on the basis of her heads of 'exotic peoples'. However, he was at pains to warn the reader: 'Miss Gordine is not yet, of course, Maillol, or even Frank Dobson and no woman could ever do the sculpture of Epstein.'[v] R R Tatlock, critic of the *Daily Telegraph*, was equally impressed in October 1928 by Gordine's 'exotic' portraits, especially 'the extraordinarily sensitively expressed' *Guadeloupe Head / Negress,* (cat no. 28) and for the massive *Mongolian Head* (1928, cat no. 32) and *Head of a Chinaman* in which the artist displays 'quite apart from her sense of plastic beauty, a distinct gift for portraiture.' Like Wilenski, he was convinced that Gordine should in future concentrate on producing portrait heads of exotic races.[vi]

Why then was there such lively contemporary interest in so-called 'exotic' peoples which enabled Gordine as a relative unknown to the British art scene to be given such as positive reception? The British and French Colonial Empires attained their territorial zenith after the First World War. The British Empire, by 1922, covered nearly 14 million square miles incorporating a population of over 500 million people.[vii] Both governments attempted to promote a greater awareness among the home populations of the peoples far away they controlled and whose raw materials they exploited. In Britain, the Conservative Government of Stanley Baldwin, seeking to promote a feeling of solidarity among the classes at home, provided considerable financial backing for the British Empire Exhibition at Wembley which opened in April 1924. It was judged such a success that an expanded version opened in April

far left:
Fig. 11 Dora Gordine
Malay Head, 1931
Catalogue only

left:
Fig. 12 Dora Gordine
Kwa Nin – Chinese Lady of Peace / Chinese Head, 1928
Catalogue only

right:
32 Dora Gordine
Mongolian Head, 1928

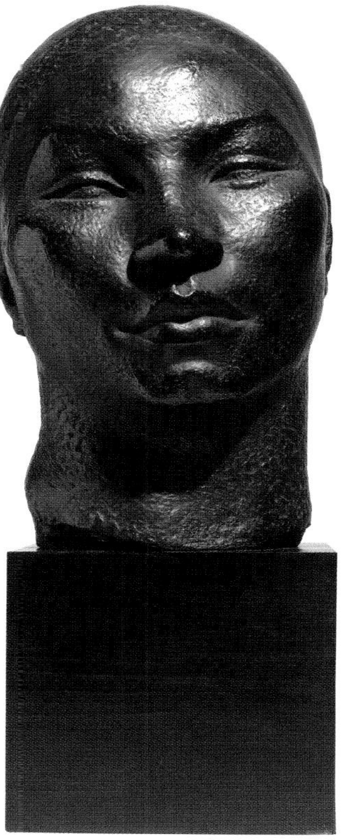

the following year. In July 1926 the government sought to capitalise on the interest aroused in the Empire by the two exhibitions by establishing the Empire Marketing Board – with a brief to promote for domestic consumption goods and materials produced by Britain's Imperial possessions – especially the so-called 'less-developed' ones in Africa and South East Asia (i.e. what was then known as Malaya).[viii]

This was also an era of best-selling books exploring the contact between Western European male officials – soldiers, pilots, engineers, geographers and explorers and the colonised, or soon to be colonised, exotic 'other' in Africa and Asia such as T E Lawrence's *Seven Pillars of Wisdom* (published in December 1926 and issued in abridged form as *Revolt in the Desert* in March 1927); André Malraux's fictionalised account of strife between Nationalist and Communist Chinese in *Les Conquérants* (published 1928) followed by his *La Voie Royale* (1930), set in the jungles of Cambodia in French Indo-China, while Antoine de Saint Exupéry wrote of his adventures with trigger-happy Berber tribesmen while flying over the North African desert in *Courrier-Sud* (1928).

Reviewers of the heads of racial types Gordine exhibited at the Leicester Galleries in October 1928, and in Berlin during September-October 1929, also remarked on her skill at patination – the dexterity with which she infused colour into the surfaces of her bronzes.[ix] Often the sitter could be made to appear all the more alien and different to the eyes of a white Western European because of the patina given to the bronze head (i.e. the patina of *Mongolian Head* makes the head appear much blacker and darker than the skin colour of an individual from that country). The same could be said of *Guadeloupe Head* and of *African Head*. The patination Gordine achieved, with the help of the Parisian foundry of Valsuani, essentially induces the white spectator to be all the more conscious of their European 'whiteness' and of the extent of the gulf separating them from the world viewed by the sitter. This was, of course, the period when Paris and to a lesser extent London, was swept by a wave of 'négrophilie' triggered in Paris by the first performances of Joséphine Baker and the *Revue Nègre* in October 1925.[x]

Early in 1930, after experiencing success in Paris, London and Berlin, Gordine left for British Malaya and Singapore. After nearly six months working in an *attap* studio, made from palm fronds, on the outskirts of Johore Bahru, capital of the Unfederated Malay State of Johore (i.e. the state was still technically independent though its ruler, the rich, self-assured and opinionated Sultan Ibrahim, was expected to heed the counsel of a British General Adviser) she told a local newspaper that in Europe '…she always felt cramped and thought of going to Africa, or the East. Later she decided on the East for here she felt sure she could find ideal types to model… She said that the naturally graceful movements of the Eastern peoples fascinated her. She contrasted

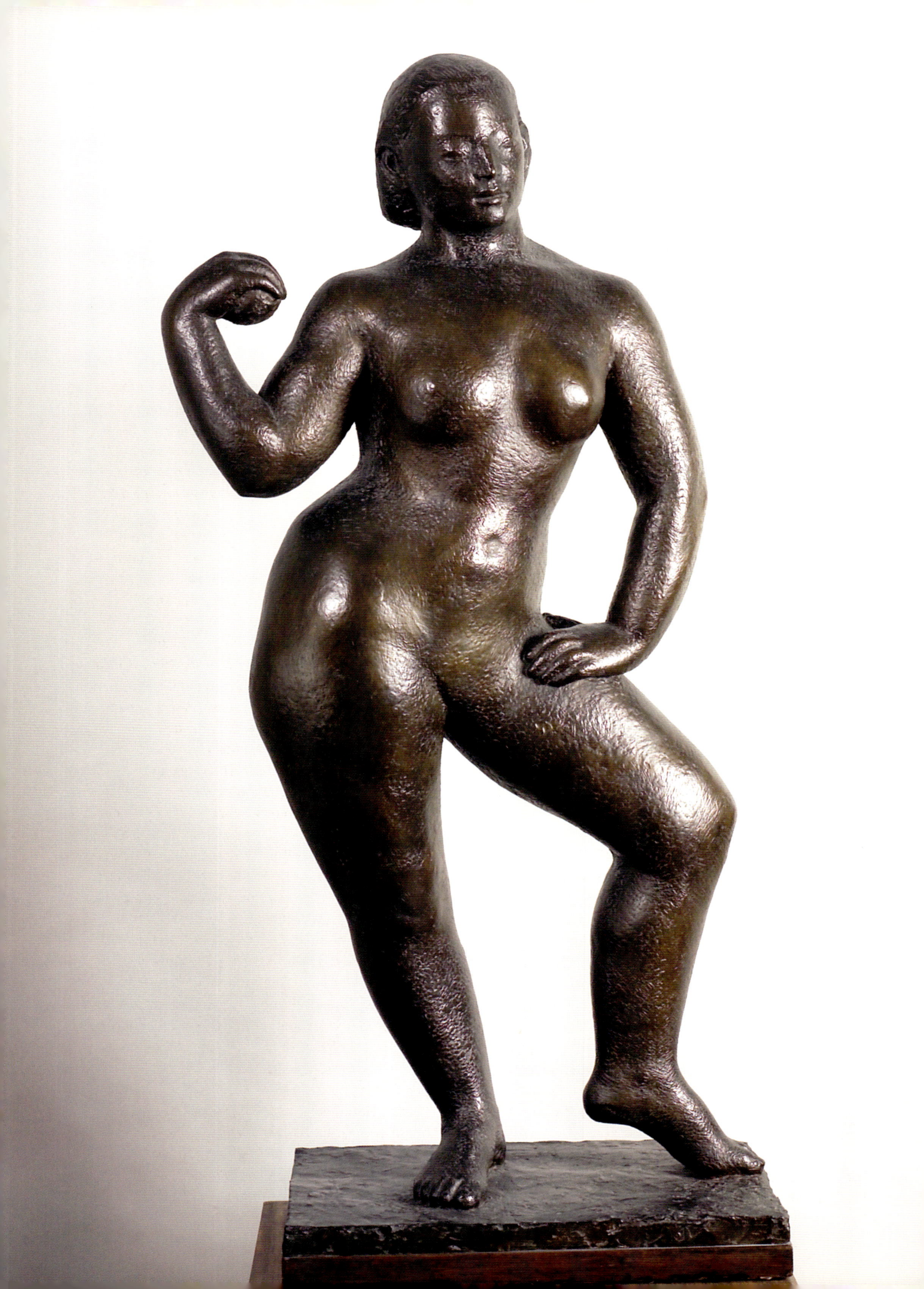

30 Dora Gordine
Javanese Dancer, 1927

the efforts the average European has to make to maintain a dignified appearance and the quiet and naturally dignified bearing of the Eastern. The figures of the Tamils, she said, are ideal for her work, for their excellent proportions and grace of line express a beauty unknown in Europe. Work is a little difficult here, she admitted, for she has not yet become accustomed to the heat… She is at present studying Hindu classic poses in the nude… Why is the East noted for its art, except because here one has the large atmosphere necessary to nourish art? Could the monuments of the Golden Hindu era to be seen in Borobudhur [a massive Buddhist temple complex on Java] and the art treasures of Angkor [in Cambodia] ever have been produced in the narrow confines of a teeming city? I am enthralled by the East, fascinated by its movement, but cannot help deploring the western influences which tend to kill its natural beauty.'[xi]

Shortly after giving this interview Gordine was approached by the Singapore Municipal Commissioners to provide suitable works for the interior of the recently opened imposing Singapore Municipal Buildings. The *Straits Times* reported: 'It has now been decided finally that Singapore is to have some examples of Dora Gordine's work and it is for the first time in the history of the Colony that the acquisition of a subject of pure art has been realised. The Municipal Offices will hold the new works in bronze. Two heads of racial types will be in the hall at the top of the great exterior steps and two more on the floor above which is next to the Council Chamber. An over-life-size torso [*Torso/Walking Male Torso*] will stand in the middle of the space there which overlooks the sea. The torso, which was taken from a Caucasian model, shows the ideal male form with broad shoulders and small hips. Two years ago the Colonial Office purchased this figure for the University of Accra where it now stands in a hall overlooking the sea, a very similar position to the one proposed here. The dynamic force, the suggestion of movement, of activity, in this bronze torso was remarked by the critics in London, Paris and Berlin. The *Mongolian Head*… has been chosen to pair with… a Malayan race head (cat no. 44) which like the Mongolian Head is heroic in size … A Chinese female head [also known as *Kwa Nin – Chinese Goddess of Peace*] (Fig. 12) of remarkable beauty – a thoughtful Madonna – and an Indian Head (now known as *Hindu Head*), which shows the probable origin of the Western classic type will complete the scheme. For the Council Chamber a fifth head is contemplated but not yet decided upon It is probable that the Chinese Female Head will be placed in the Council Chamber.'[xii] The Commissioners largely took this unprecedented step of buying and commissioning art for the Municipal Buildings because the British were attempting to foster a sense of Malayan national identity among the racially divided peoples who composed the population of the peninsula and on Singapore Island i.e. the Malays; the Chinese (in charge of business and banking); Indians – themselves divided between Hindu Tamils imported to work on the rubber plantations and Sikhs who predominated in the Police Service as well as recent immigrants from Dutch-controlled Java and Sumatra. At the top of the pyramid were the white British and at the bottom the indigenous, aboriginal nomadic tribes people usually known as Dyaks.[xiii]

Gordine's cause was championed by Richard Winstedt, General Adviser to Johore from 1931-35. By the time of the Singapore Municipal Buildings commission, she was ironically able to present herself as less of an overtly 'exotic' or alien individual. In September 1930 she became a British citizen by marrying Dr. George Herbert Garlick then Deputy, and later Director, of the Johore Medical Service. She had obviously arrived within colonial society in Johore and on Singapore Island as her wedding reception was attended by no less than the Sultan of Johore's sister (a future sitter for a portrait head), one of the Sultan's brothers, the Sultan's Deputy Prime Minister and by Winstedt's predecessor as General Adviser. During 1931-32 Gordine toured French Indo-China, Thailand and the Dutch East Indies. She indeed inspected those sites she had singled out for praise in her September 1930 interview: Borobudhur in Java and Angkor Wat in French-controlled Cambodia. In August 1932 she sailed for Paris and then London where she held an exhibition of her latest works in July 1933 at the Leicester Galleries.

This exhibition was dominated by pieces inspired by her time in South-East Asia and by the stone carvings she had closely scrutinsied at Angkor Wat and Borobudhur such as the compelling portrait heads of *A Malay Sultana, The Tungku Ampuan of Johore* (1932,

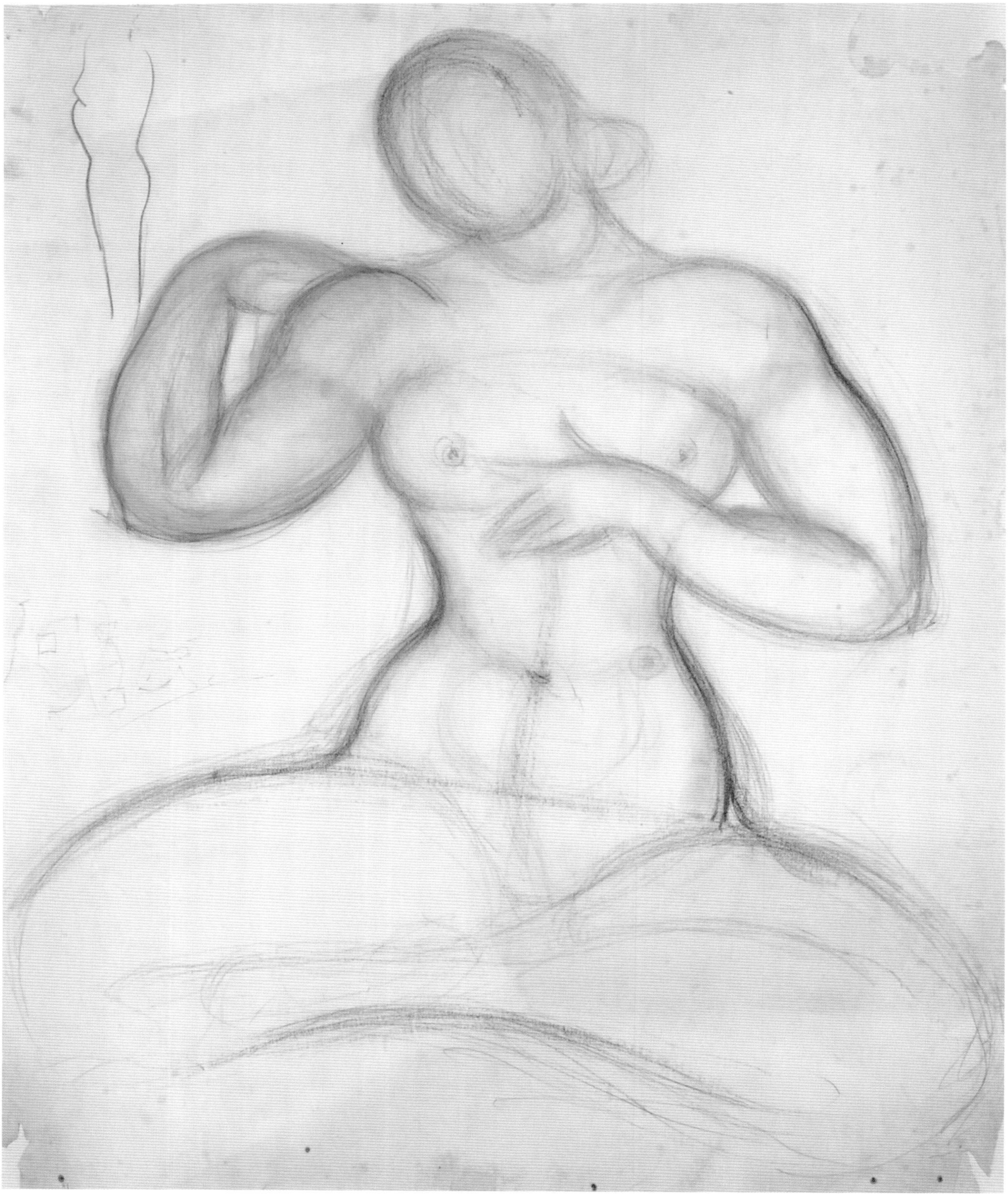

40 Dora Gordine
Study for Pagan I, c. 1933

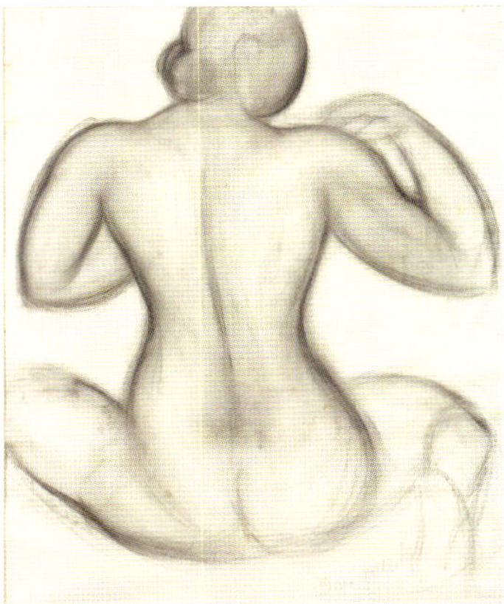

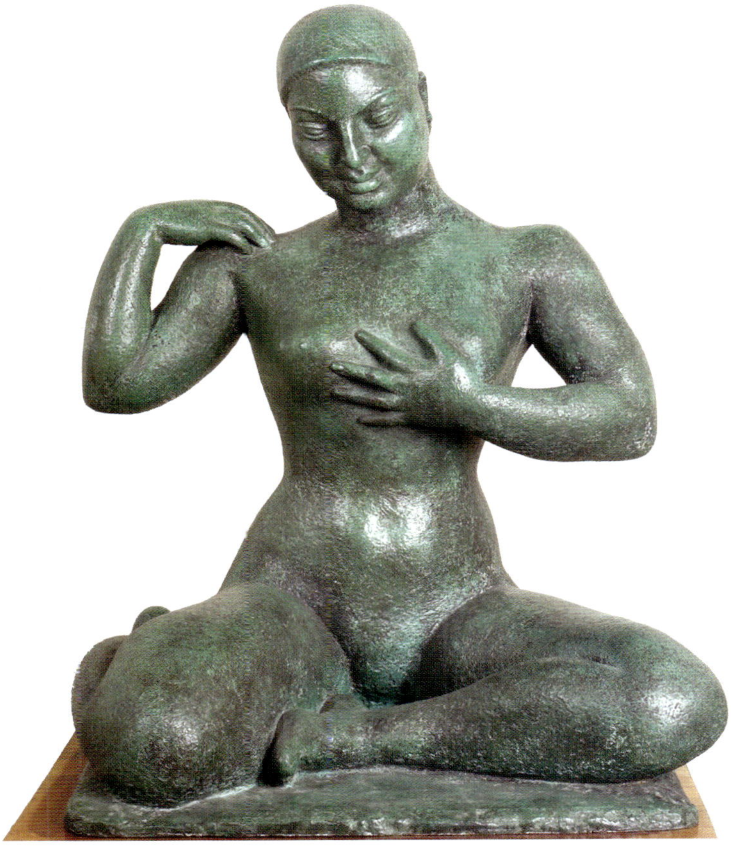

above:
41 Dora Gordine
Study for Pagan II, c.1933

left:
Fig. 13 Dora Gordine
Pagan / Femina, 1933
Catalogue only

cat no. 44); *Javanese Head* (cat no. 35); *Hindu Head; Malay Head* and the female Chinese head known as *Kwa Nin*, as well as larger figures such as: *Male Torso / Dyak* (Fig. 14), the sensual yet remote *Pagan* (Fig. 13) and *Cingalese Girl.*

The critics were greatly taken with this superb selection of racial heads. They existed as non-threatening types. Gordine did not give them specific individualising names. They are presented as and defined by labels devised by Western European explorers, anthropologists and ethnographers; they are 'Mongolian', 'Malay', 'Hindu Indian' or 'African'; apart from their sex no further information is supplied as to their tribe, caste, age or their particular area of origin within a wider geographical location invariably supplied with a name coined in the West but usually unrecognised by those who actually live there. Paradoxically, Epstein often provided the first name of his non-white sitters i.e. *Sunita* (cat no. 20) and *Rani* (cat no. 24) and yet, far more than is the case with Gordine, one is aware in his work of the overt intervention of the artist – of the action of his fingers and thumbs. Looking at an Epstein head of a non-white sitter from within the British Empire, one is aware first and foremost that one is contemplating an Epstein with all its trademark bravura handling of the clay.

The Morning Post's critic thought Gordine had definitely improved and that her status had even risen with regard to Epstein: 'The search for character is more profound and her craftsmanship has reached a degree of subtlety and emotional fervour which one misses from Epstein's oeuvre. Moreover, her sense of colour is remarkable as she shows in the … lovely and varied patina which distinguishes the different pieces on view. It fascinates one to watch the light play over the sensitive modelling of face and figure, revealing here an accent, there a new movement in the direction of rhythm, or of surface technique, all combining to express outward beauty and strength and inward power, grace and feeling.' The heads and figures were sensuous and beguiling rather than confrontationally powerful. The feminine figures were charming rather than disturbingly overtly eroticised: 'an Eastern charm lurks in the lively curves of the *Cingalese Girl*'.[xiv] Frank Rutter, in *The Sunday Times*, also mentioned Epstein in connection with Gordine: '… Miss Gordine has a good deal in common with Mr Epstein, not only does she seem to prefer Asiatics to Europeans as models… she is essen-

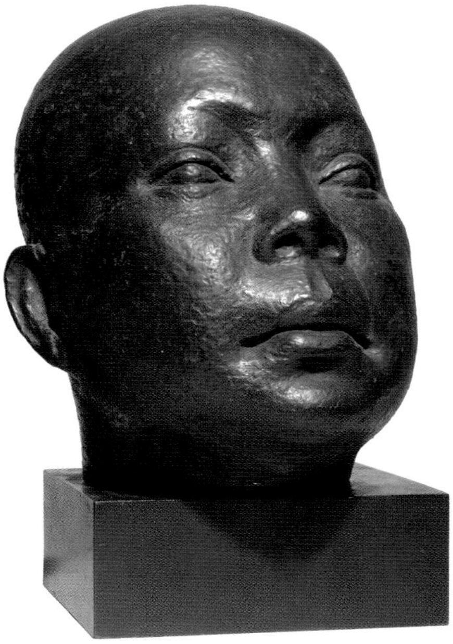

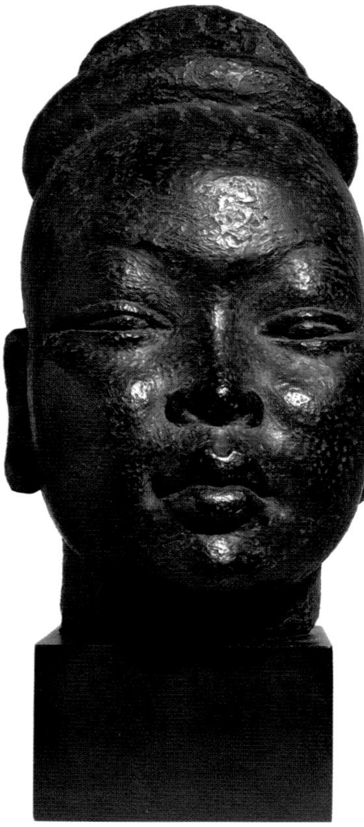

left:
44 Dora Gordine
A Malay Sultana (The Tungku Ampuan of Johore), 1932

right:
35 Dora Gordine
Javanese Head, 1931

tially a modeller rather than a carver. Also her heads usually are more entirely successful than her full-length figures … Her *Head of a Chinese Lady* [*Kwa Nin*] is well-nigh perfect in beauty of subject and treatment while the astounding mastery of her modelling is seen in her *Javanese Head* in which – to take one feature only – the sensitively modelled lips seem to be positively quivering with life. Again, like Mr Epstein, Miss Gordine can most conveniently be classed as a romantic sculptor …'[xv]

The most impassioned vindication of Gordine's perspective on exoticism was offered by Arthur Symons – the former Symbolist poet and one-time friend of Oscar Wilde. He seemed to feel that, as a Russian, Gordine's 'genius … is primitive and passionate; there is an inexplicable strain of virility combined with youth, fascination and wisdom. She feels in her blood the power of Russian music and that explains the harmonious rhythm of her sculpture.'[xvi] According to Symons: ' … the flesh for her … appeals to her primitive soul … ' Symons also described *Male Torso / Dyak* as '… magnificently masculine and there is an intense simplicity and that intensity of life which seems to exist in every limb. She [Gordine] has given him neither head nor feet. What she gives is the body of a primitive animal, ready to seize his prey like a wild beast, virile and capable of any violent action. And you feel the solidity of that immense weight, what force and reality, what sudden arrested life [is] in those long arms and furiously clenched hands.'[xvii]

The works directly informed by her first stay in South-East Asia, exhibited in July 1933, proved to be the high watermark of her involvement with the racially colonised exotic. She returned to Malaya in the autumn of 1933 but devoted much of her time to sketching the temple dancers of Bali – itself now an established part of the tourist circuit for the wealthy.[xviii] Two years later she divorced Dr. Garlick, sailed for London and married the English aristocrat the Hon Richard Hare. It is most noticeable that the majority of the portrait heads she exhibited at her next successful show, at the Leicester Galleries in November 1938, depicted British males who belonged to the nation's social, cultural, economic and political elites i.e. *Lord Glenconner* (chairman of Charles Tennant and Sons and of the British Oil Development Company, with drilling rights in Iraq and Saudi Arabia); *D S MacColl* (art critic and former Keeper of the Wallace

Collection), *Sir Harry Sheil Vanderpant* (Lord Mayor of Westminster) and *H S Goodhart Rendel* (President of the RIBA 1937-39). It is possible that Gordine sensed that the days of easy living for the British in the Far East were decidedly numbered as their casually assumed racial superiority, resting upon deceptively impressive military foundations, was challenged by the aggressively expansionist Empire of Japan.[xix]

In addition, married to Richard Hare, Gordine was part of a politically left-leaning milieu that regarded the British Empire with discomfort rather than with pride. Indeed, shortly after the Second World War, her brother-in-law by marriage, the Earl of Listowel, played a key role in supervising the withdrawal of British power from first India (1947) and then Burma (1948) as Colonial Secretary in the Labour government of Clement Attlee.[xx] As the Empire gave way to a new Commonwealth, Gordine eagerly prepared to encounter and visually chronicle faces belonging to a new and even more glitteringly insidious form of visual exoticism: Hollywood.

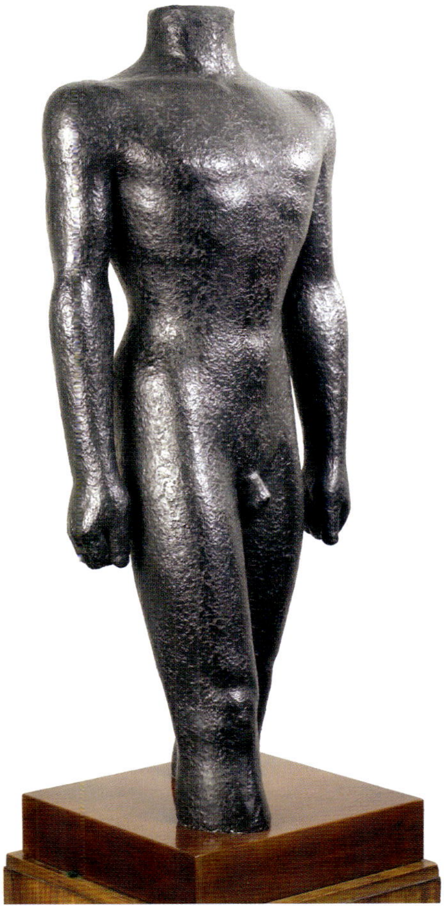

Fig. 14 Dora Gordine
Dyak / Man / Headhunter, 1932

[i] *Le Crapouillot* 1927, p.11
[ii] Gordine later revealed that the man's name was Chia Chu Chung and that he was an art critic studying philosophy at the Sorbonne *The Straits Times*, 12 August 1930, p.14
[iii] Olivier Todd, *Malraux: A Life* (New York: Alfred A. Knopf, 2005), pp.65-68
[iv] Gerald Reitlinger in *Drawing and Design*, February 1928, p.59
[v] R H Wilenski in *The Evening Standard*, 5 October 1928, Dorich House Archives [henceforth DHA]
[vi] R R Tatlock in *The Daily Telegraph*, 6 October 1928, p.15
[vii] Niall Ferguson, *Empire: How Britain Made The Modern World* (London: Penguin, 2004), Chapter Six
[viii] For the impact of the 1924 and 1925 Wembley exhibitions see: Cathy Ross, *Twenties London: A City in the Jazz Age* (London: Philip Wilson Publishers, 2003), pp.72-78
[ix] *Dorfische Zeitung* (Berlin), 23 September 1929, DHA
[x] Petrine Archer-Shaw, *Negrophilia: Avant-Garde Paris and Black Culture in the 1920s* (London: Thames & Hudson, 2000)
[xi] *The Straits Times*, 12 August 1930, p.14
[xii] *The Straits Times*, 30 January 1931, p.12
[xiii] Margaret Shennan *Out In The Midday Sun: The British In Malaya 1880-1960* (London: John Murray, 2004), Chapters 7 and 8
[xiv] *The Morning Post*, 5 July 1933, DHA
[xv] *The Sunday Times*, 9 July 1933, p.7
[xvi] *The Spectator*, 14 July 1933, p.A5
[xvii] Ibid., p.A6
[xviii] John Keay, *Last Post: The End of Empire in the Far East* (London: John Murray, 2005), p.14
[xix] Ibid., p.139
[xx] Peter Hennessy, *Never Again: Britain 1945-1951* (London: Vintage, 1993), pp.229-235

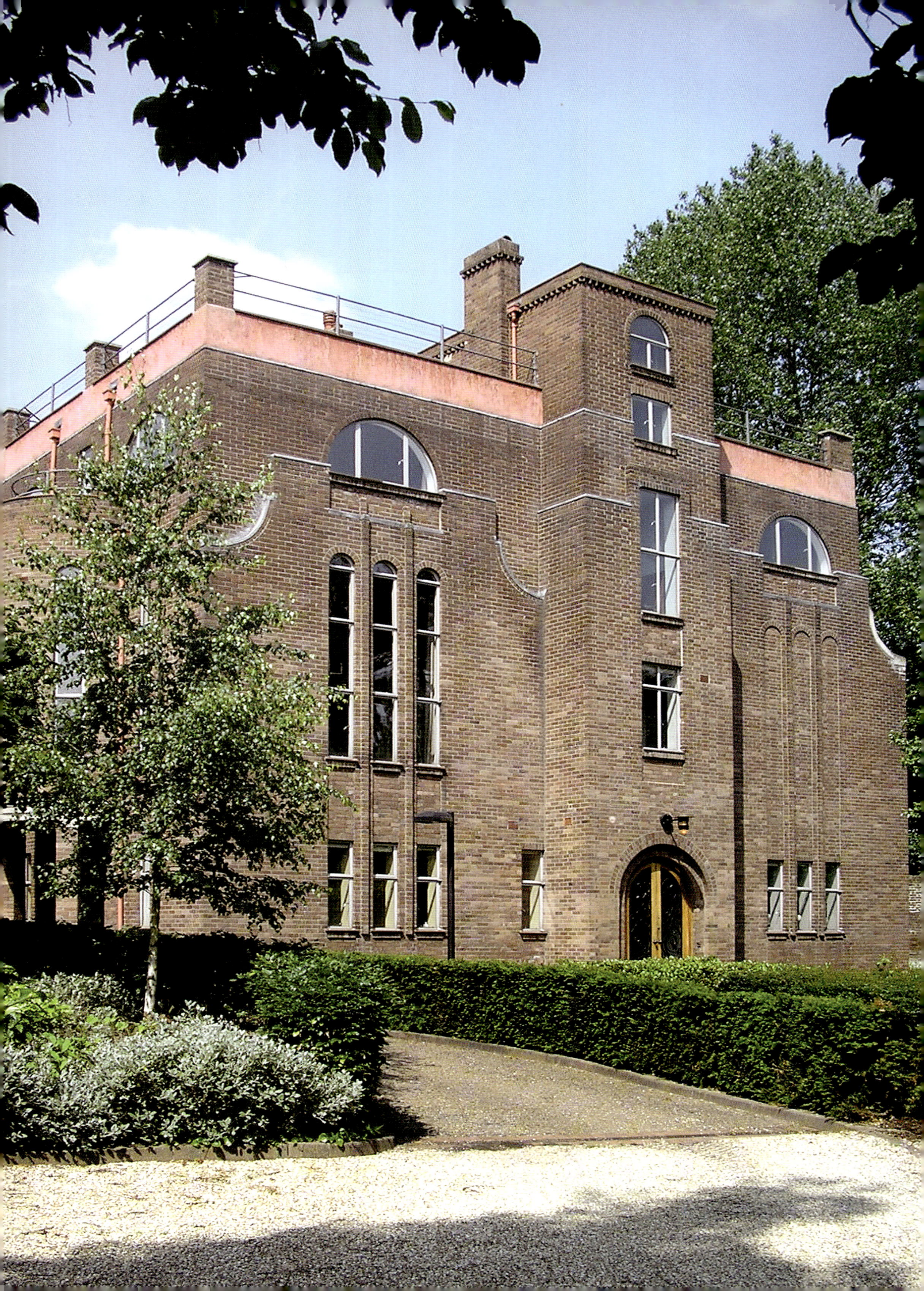

An Artist at Home:

Studio Residences and Dora Gordine

Brenda Martin

Curator, Dorich House, Kingston University

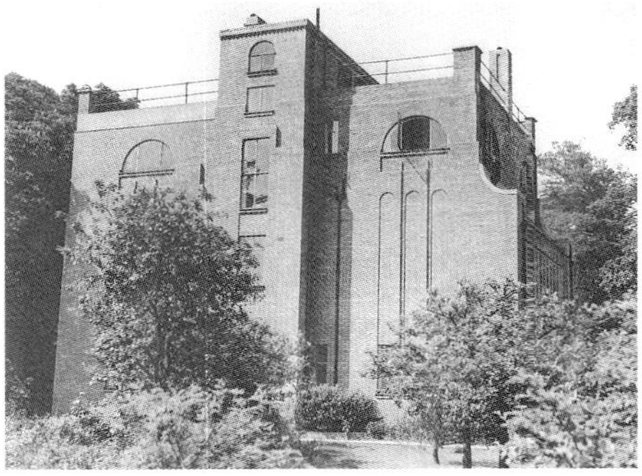

Brenda Martin is the Curator of the Dorich House Museum at Kingston University and a Design Historian. Research interests focus on the interiors and architecture of the 1920s and 1930s, and on the design work of Dora Gordine. Recent publications are *Dora Gordine Sculpture Collection, Dorich House Museum, Kingston University* (Dorset: Bond & Coyne, 2005), 'A House of her Own' in *Women's Places, Architecture and Design 1860-1960* (Ed. with Professor Penny Sparke, London and New York: Routledge, 2003), and 'Photographs of a Legacy' in *The Modern Period Room: The Construction of the Exhibited Interior 1870-1950* (Ed. with Dr. Trevor Keeble, Professor Penny Spake, London and New York: Routledge, forthcoming May 2006) She is also responsible for instituting and convening the Dorich House Annual Conference.

left:
Fig. 15 *Dorich House*, 2005

above:
Fig. 16 *Dorich House*, 1936

I put all my soul, my vitality, joy of life, movement and gaiety into my work.
I often feel that if people want to know me they should
look at my sculpture because words are not my medium at all.
It is sculpture that is my medium.

So said the Estonian sculptor Dora Gordine (1898-1991) when she was interviewed by Nancy Wise for BBC Radio in 1972 for the series *A Second Home*, a programme in which émigrés talked about their lives in their adopted homelands.[i] By that time, Dora Gordine had been living in England since 1935 and had married a peer of the realm in 1936, the Hon. Richard Hare (1907-1966). Hare's substantial inheritance had financed the building for her of Dorich House, a superb studio residence on three floors, on the edge of Richmond Park, London SW15. Dorich House – a conflation of their two first names – was designed by Gordine at the pinnacle of her success and it embodied all her social and professional aspirations. Her husband, Richard Hare, was a brilliant scholar who graduated from Oxford with a first class degree in Politics, Philosophy and Economics in 1929, and entered the diplomatic service. After the war, he became an academic specialising in Russian Literature and Art at the School of Eastern European Studies at the University of London. He was an avid collector and patron of the arts, an activity which supported his ambition to leave his impressive and rare collection of Imperial Russian art to the British nation.[ii] Conceived by Gordine to provide studios and a gallery to showcase her sculpture and the Russian collection, Dorich House can be seen as an expression of the exotic and bohemian identity of its owner (Figs. 15 and 16).

Born in the Imperial Russian province of Latvia, probably to a wealthy Jewish family, Dora Gordine started life in a country which at its southern borders joined with Turkey, Kazakhstan, Mongolia and China and where the onion shaped domes of its churches proclaim an affinity with Asian architectural forms rather than the pointed spires of European Gothic. Through these ancient borderlands the Asian love of jewel-like colours spread through Russia influencing the folk art and traditional costumes of the Boyars. The joy of life and the sensuality of the Arabian tales which are gathered in the publication *The Thousand Nights and One Night* are matched in the Russian fairytales which Gordine remembered being told in childhood, a time she described as:

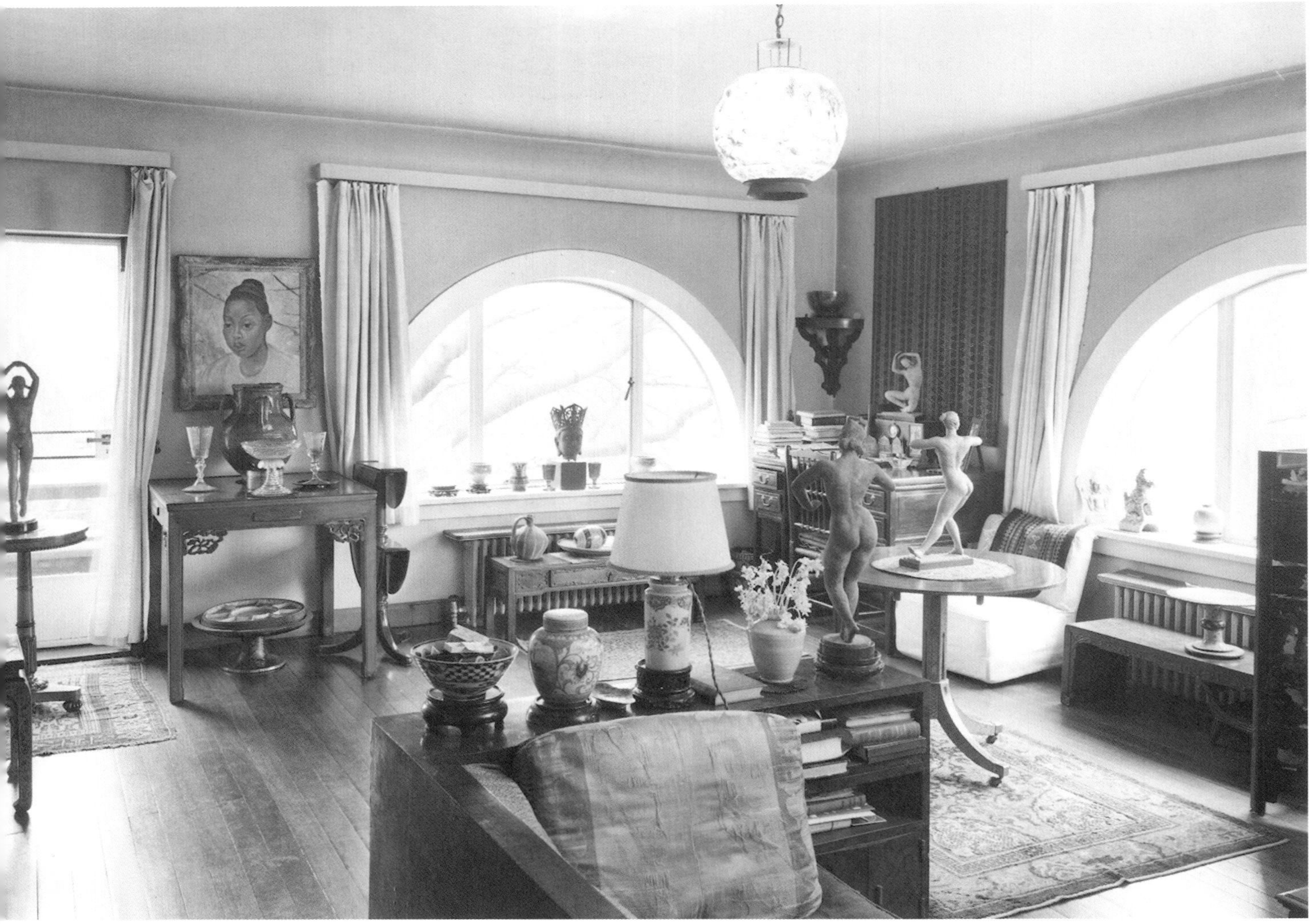

Fig. 17 *The Sitting Room at Dorich House,* c.1949

> *a sparkling life with a lot of beauty around me. There were many fairytales which give a wonderful feeling of seeing life through the smoke of fairy tales.*[iii]

Vitality, joy of life and gaiety are perhaps the very things which attracted Gordine to the great ancient civilisations and peoples of Asia, India and China.

In the aftermath of the Russian Revolution the Gordine family relocated to Berlin and subsequently Gordine arrived alone in Paris to study art. She claims not to have attended art school, but to have studied the collections at the Louvre and those at the lesser known Musée Cernuschi, specialists in the Asian, Oriental and Indian Arts.[iv] In 1925 Gordine worked as a painter at the *Exposition Internationale des Arts Décoratifs and Industriels Modernes* where she would have encountered first hand the modern decorative interpretations of the exotic that were the foundations of the 'art deco' style. The exotic dancer, Joséphine Baker was appearing in the *Revue Nègre* at the Champs Elysées, and at the Cernuschi, the big exhibition in 1925 was *Siamese and Cambodian Statuary*. That the ancient Khmer statues influenced Gordine's work can never be in doubt once one has seen Gordine's bronze *Iran / Goddess of Health* made in 1933. The celebrated sculptor, Aristide Maillol, encouraged Gordine to continue to study alone to develop her emerging talent. Interestingly, she later told the sculpture conservators from the Tate Gallery in 1990, that when she met Maillol during her early years in Paris she was working as a decorator.[v] Gordine's design work stands alongside her sculpture as an important part of her oeuvre and, although it would be 1936 before she designed Dorich House, the building has two influential antecedents. The first was a studio house by Auguste Perret for Gordine in Boulogne-Billancourt in Paris in 1929 and the second was a studio house by Godfrey Samuel on the edge of Hampstead Heath in London in 1934.

The studio house in Paris was built following considerable artistic success for Gordine, which started with *Chinese Head/Chinaman/Chinese Philosopher*, exhibited in 1926 at the Salon des Tuileries. Further commercial success followed from portraits and an exhibition at the Leicester Galleries in London in 1928. Like the Ukranian sculptor, Chana Orloff, Margaret Huré, the glass painter who created the windows for Perret's church of *Notre Dame du Raincy* and the Polish artist, Maria Melania Mutermilch (Mela Muter) Gordine commissioned Perret, who was a neighbour and friend, to build her a 'modern' studio.[vi] She chose an area which had many individual studios and private houses built in the 1920s and 1930s for a growing artistic colony, specifically designed by modernist architects of the day such as Le Corbusier, Robert Mallet Stevens and Tony Garnier. Her brief to Perret showed her priorities in life and the choice of Perret as the architect could well have been because his studios are noted for his attention to detail and for fulfilling the programme of his clients as a first priority.[vii] On the ground floor was a plaster studio and storage for the plasters. On the middle floor, Perret designed an adjacent double height modelling studio and gallery space, with interconnecting doors providing long vistas to see new pieces of sculpture. In the modelling studio was a raised platform area, so that Dora could look at her sculpture from the floor, because, as she said later:

> *for me the most important thing is to work from the floor, and [to] look at the sculpture from below … people have no idea what the person looks like really, or what inspires you to do it – pure form, voluptuousness, a susceptible smile – seen from below. When you look at things from the floor it is unbelievable – everything is round and big like a mountain – if you want to see the real shape of the mountain you need to go to the bottom and not look at it from afar.*[viii]

The north wall of the studio consisted entirely of a large expanse of windows which must have flooded the studio with a steady northern light. The elegant top floor apartment was flooded with daylight too, with the living rooms and kitchen having large glass doors which opened out to a terrace.

For the interiors, Gordine set simple furniture against the pale grey and white walls, which show little evidence of occupation in the few photographs that we have of the time. Completed in late 1929, it is doubtful whether she lived in the Paris studio for long as it seems to have been completed while Gordine was in Berlin for her exhibition at the Flechtheim Gallery. Gordine went directly from Berlin to Singapore for the Municipal Buildings commission in late 1929/1930, (elaborated on in an essay elsewhere in this catalogue by Dr Jonathan Black), returning in 1933 to prepare work for an exhibition at the Salon des Tuileries.

Gordine's next venture into the province of architectural design remains a tantalising and intriguing episode. Shortly after arriving in Singapore, she married Dr G H Garlick, a doctor for the Sultan of Johore. Although they would have been provided with quarters in the Malay royal compound, it seems that the couple also built a house together in Singapore. The area was bought by BP Petroleum in the 1960s and the house demolished. However, local colleagues of Dr Garlick and architectural tutors from the local technical college remember their house as being completely round 'like a drum', and built on principles of Straits Chinese architecture, with a central atrium which is covered by, but not joined to, a large overhanging roof, to facilitate the flow of cooling air through the living spaces. The three floors were linked by a spiral staircase to one side. Daylight was provided by sets of three tall windows at regular intervals. A colleague of Gordine's first husband recalls that the house was designed by her and that it was filled with her sculpture, both in the garden and outside. Possibly Gordine's preference for rounded sensuous forms, clearly evident in her sculpture, also found expression in her architectural designs. In the Garlick house in Singapore she took inspiration from the vernacular architecture of the Straits Chinese and added her own passion for the convex to the extreme. Research continues into the whereabouts of the plans for the Garlick house and for local photographs.

In February 1934 Richard Hare visited Gordine in Singapore while he was travelling around South East Asia. Hare had recently presented *Javanese Head* (cat no. 30) from Gordine's 1933 exhibition at the Leicester Galleries to the Tate collection. By then the Garlick marriage was presumably in trouble, since Hare wrote to London to his old school friend, Godfrey Samuel, a modernist architect and partner in Tecton (one of the few modern architectural practices which were using reinforced concrete in their houses) asking him to buy a plot of land for Gordine from the Highgate Lodge estate, which was being sold off by Sir Arthur Crosfield on the edge of Hampstead Heath in North London.[ix] Letters between Hare, Samuel and Gordine from 1934 and 1935, concerning the design of a studio home by Samuel for Gordine, reveal how deeply Gordine had been affected by the exotic architecture of Singapore and Malaya, particularly with regard to the use of daylight. Samuel submitted several designs for a studio house, which, like the Paris studio, would provide two working studios and a gallery, with domestic accommodation in a modern style using the latest materials and techniques available at the time. The approved design was for one large square building in a

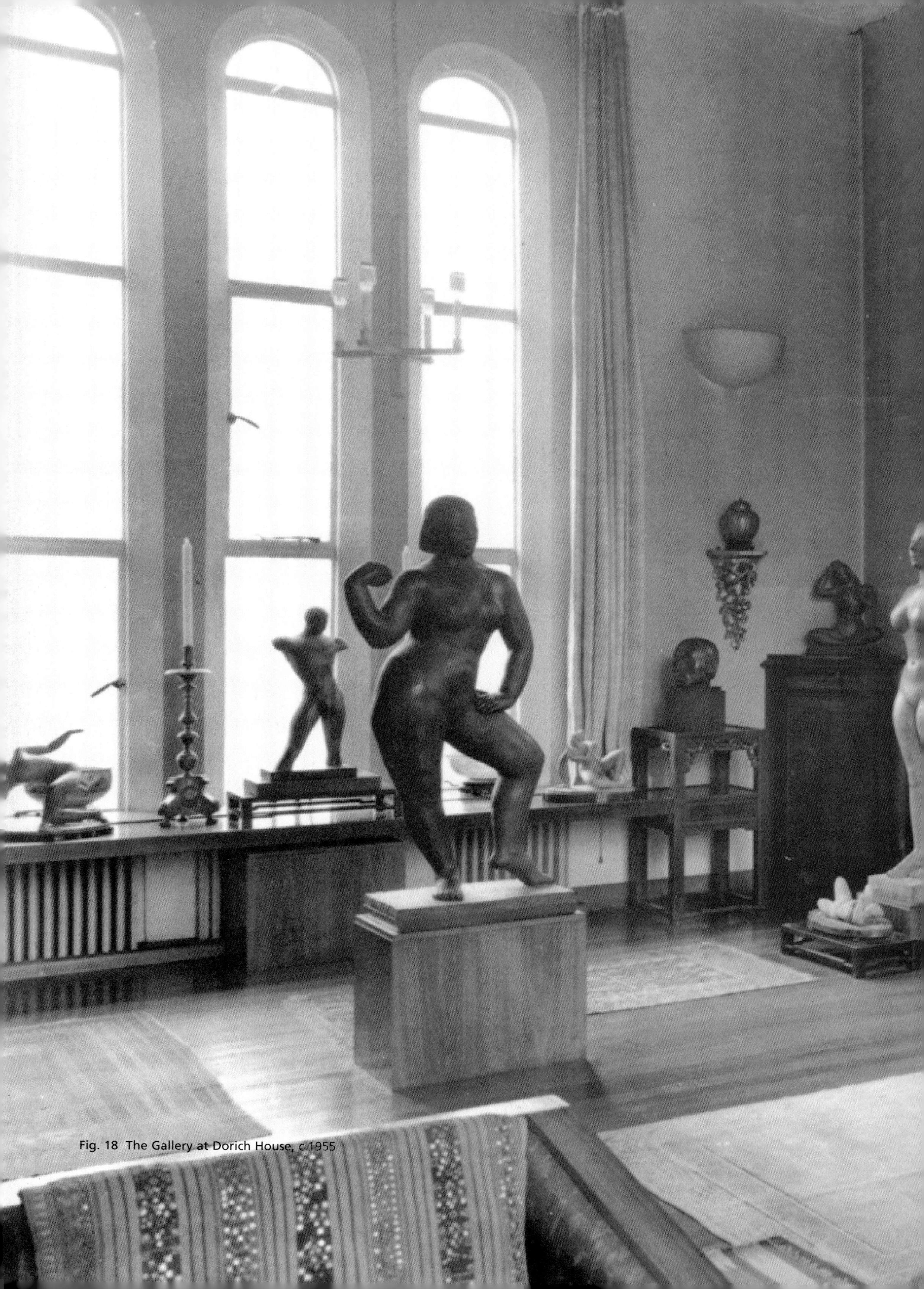

Fig. 18 The Gallery at Dorich House, c.1955

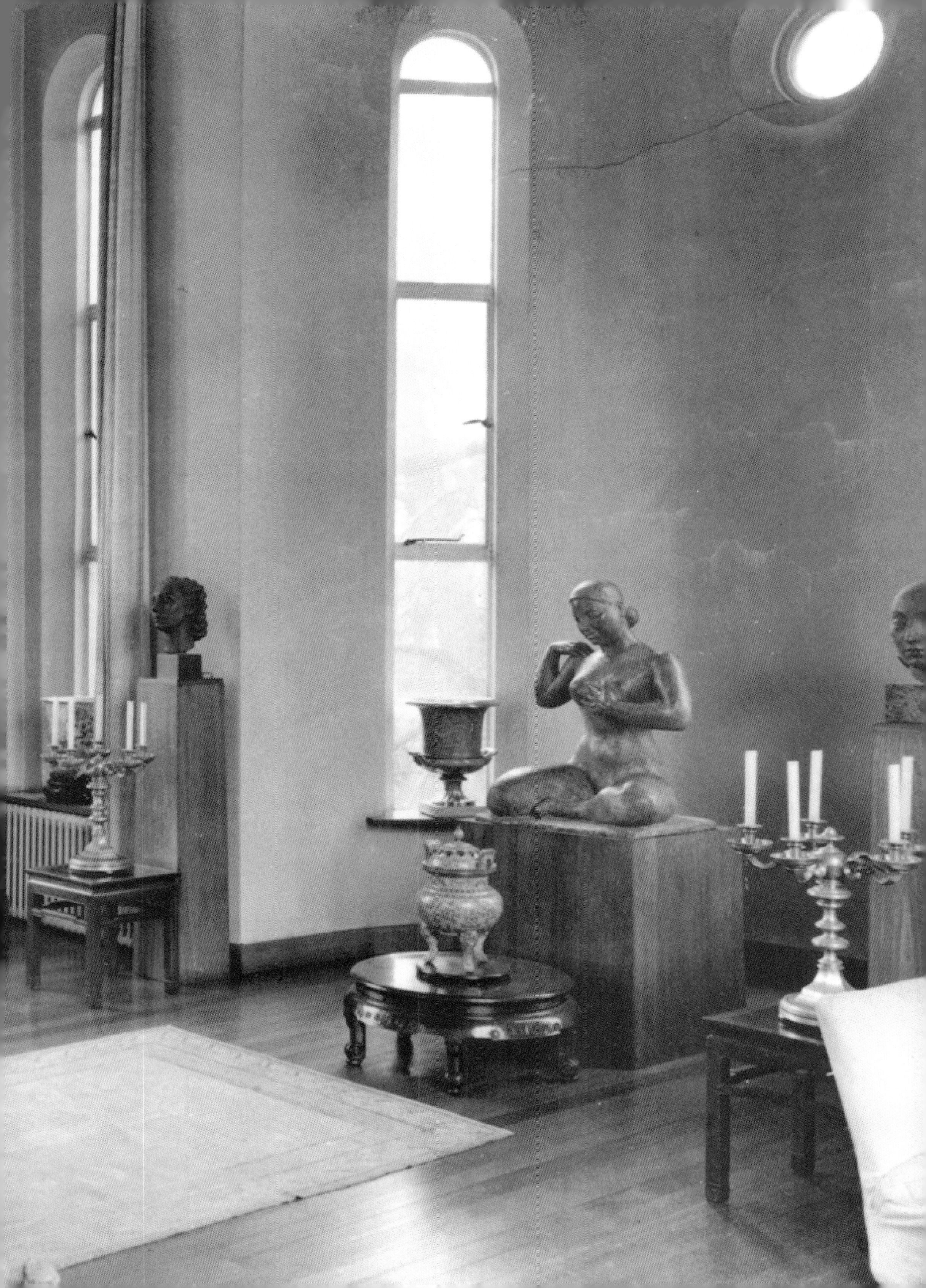

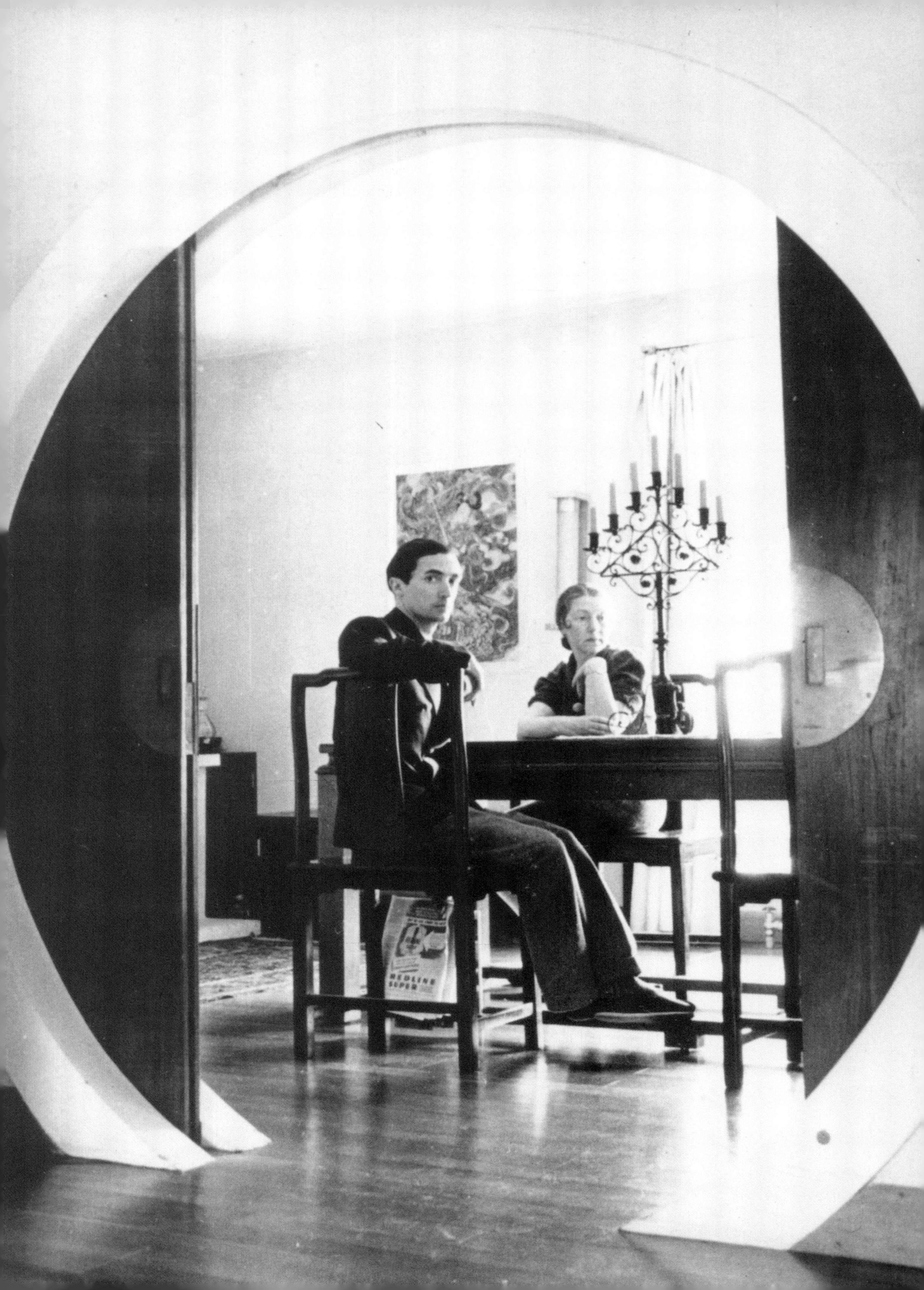

Fig. 19 *The Chinese Moon Door at Dorich House with Dora Gordine and Richard Hare at the dining table,* c.1949

severely Modernist style which, in June 1935, was refused planning permission as being too modern for the picturesque area of Hampstead and Highgate.

The project failed, but their correspondence reveals Gordine's criticisms of the design and her suggestions for alternatives. For example, when Samuel suggested large fig glass windows in the south wall of the gallery, Gordine was appalled, and replied that large windows would admit too much light for the display of sculpture, suggesting instead that sets of three narrow round topped windows would light the sculptures better. Samuel replied disparagingly that the effect would be that of a 'Chelsea front drawing room'. In the pale sun of England, he could not imagine that his client was perhaps influenced by the exotic architecture of the Straits Chinese, where the vernacular architecture of the traditional 'shop house' has narrow windows with curved tops to limit the glare and heat of a fierce sun, creating a cool and shady space within. Until the 1880s these houses would have been built by Chinese or Indian contractors relying on plans in pattern books but around the turn of the century Western architects began freely combining elements of Classical Western and Chinese architecture. By 1927 when an Architects Ordinance was passed requiring all buildings to be designed by qualified architects, departures from western classical forms were not only integrated with Chinese and Indian forms but also with a Modernist architectural aesthetic.[x] In addition to criticising the window design, Gordine suggested the inclusion of a Chinese Moon Door first for the entrance to a terrace on the west of the house, and then as a division between the two living rooms, an idea which she later realised to great effect in Dorich House. Other innovations included a request for arched doorways between some of the rooms and for the entrance into the Gallery. It is evident that the hybridity of styles which flourished in the new homes of the British colonialists of the 1930s provided Gordine with a rich source of ideas for her largest and greatest architectural project, Dorich House.

Gordine returned to England without her husband in 1935. Owing to the political situation in France it was impossible for her to return to her beautiful Paris studio and she took a flat at 60 Church Street in London. Lacking the inclination to employ another architect, and abandoning Godfrey Samuel, Dora Gordine and Richard Hare designed Dorich House themselves. In November 1936 they married at Chelsea Registry Office and shortly after moved into their new home.

The severe exterior elevations of Dorich House have an almost industrial aesthetic, while the interiors are a combination of Modernist and oriental architectural elements. They are a testament to this couple's passion for the exotic and non western. Pale grey, cream and buff colour schemes were complemented by gleaming floors made of Australian Jarrah wood. In the two studios and gallery of the first two floors, the cool aesthetic of Modernism was tempered by the highly polished gleaming tropical hardwoods that Gordine preferred for her furniture, most of which originated from Singapore and China. Two huge seventeenth century Chinese cupboards, made of coramandel wood (a rich hazel-brown wood with black stripes) with circular brass locking plates provided storage, while twenty or thirty low benches and tables of oriental design were used to display smaller sculptures, oriental vases and their growing collection of Imperial Russian Art. Turkish, Persian and Indian rugs were scattered around the floors and three seventeenth century Chinese frescos were sunk into recesses in the dining room. A round lampshade decorated with Oriental figures shaded the central light (Fig. 17).

The south facing Gallery is lit to great effect as the sun moves round during the day by a series of tall narrow windows with rounded tops (Fig. 18). In a semi- circular apse at one end Gordine placed *Pagan*, a seated female bronze in an Indian pose (Fig. 18). The studio closely follows Perret's design, with a large north wall of windows which at the top are raked back to meet the recessed top floor, giving even more light to the studio. Like Perret's studio the room is of double height and has a raised dais at the Western end. For lampshades in both studios, Gordine inverted the wide cane hats of the Chinese rice workers.

In the small apartment above the studios, the interior decoration is a stunning combination of the modern and the exotic. The outstanding feature is the Chinese Moon Door (Fig. 19), made of a Malayan wood specially imported for the purpose, which divides the living and dining room. The circular proportions of the door are repeated in the semi circular windows of all the top floor rooms. A modern sofa unit, purpose-built with sliding cupboard doors of green glass and bookshelves and veneered in an exotic hardwood, designed by Gordine, stood by the fireplace. On the windowsills were displayed small statues of Buddha, Thai heads of deities, a Sino-Tibetan gilt bronze figure of an immortal riding a mule, Chinese dragons and other Chinese pots and bowls. There were Indian brass spherical lanterns, pierced with

Fig. 20 *Dora Gordine at home*, c.1939

birds and foliage. The Hares' collection of oriental art included framed and glazed textiles of silk embroidered with lotus flowers, insects and bats and wall hangings decorated with designs of dragons, figures, flowers and fans. There were two small decorative Chinese lacquered tables, coloured fabrics from Bali hung on the walls and a black lacquered screen near the fireplace with panels decorated with Chinese figures in an oriental landscape.

As one emerges onto the roof terrace, superb views over Richmond Park can be seen from a covered area, where, in hot weather, the Hares used to sleep in the open air.

Gordine said in her interview for the BBC that her visit to South East Asia was

> *a terrific affair for me. The Far East has great qualities and it was such a privilege to know those qualities. That is what made me think very deeply that one should never follow a fashion in art. Quality ... never dates – it is yesterday, today and tomorrow ... A fashion is bound to go out of fashion one day.*[xi]

Other items she brought back from her travels were the dining table and chairs, which were made from a dark Chinese hardwood. The carver chairs had a carved frieze in the Chinese style. In the hall stood two Chinese chairs of ebony inlaid with mother of pearl.

A photograph taken in the late 1930s shows Dora Gordine at her most exotic. With her stylish kiss-curl, she is standing by the window of her flat arranging some foliage from the garden in a huge old Persian Jar. The jar stands on a Chinese mahjong table where she used to play with the Tungku Ampuan of Johore, the first royal Malay princess who broke with Islamic tradition and sat for a portrait by Gordine. Behind her is a portrait of a Malay girl who was suffering from depression when Gordine first painted her. Gordine recounts the story that the girl recovered as a result of being her model and sat for a second portrait which shows her smiling happily out of the canvas[xii] (Fig. 20).

After Richard Hare's death in 1966 at the age of 59, Gordine continued to live alone in Dorich House until her death in 1991, aged 93. Although her brother, Leopold, lived in a London suburb until his death in 1979, Dora did not turn to him in old age, still preferring to deny her past and her family and to maintain a romantic and bohemian identity. A series of neighbours and chance acquaintances became friends in her later years, fascinated by her personality. They recall that she was full of character, with a sharp wit and active mind, rising early as she always had done with enormous energy and listening to the World Service on the radio until the early hours of the morning. They said that she regretted the passing of old world courtesies and the hectic pace of the modern world. She ceased actively sculpting around 1975, probably because her sight was affected by cataracts. Her last commission was the head of a grandchild of one of her neighbours on Kingston Hill. Although Dora's family was almost certainly Jewish, she did not practise the religion, but friends talk of a mystical spirituality, and more than once she claimed to have had an extraordinary gift for insight into people, a claim which is borne out by the sitters themselves.[xiii] Other evidence of Gordine's interest in the 'fourth dimension' is found in the presence of a medium at her social gatherings, something which was more acceptable in the cultures of India and the East than in the West.[xiv]

Dorich House is now a museum owned by Kingston University. The major collection of Gordine's work is displayed throughout the three floors of studios and living spaces, together with the couple's collection of Imperial Russian art. There were no children from the marriage, but Gordine always said that her sculptures were her children. The award of museum status in 2004 fulfilled the couple's lifelong ambition and their legacy lives on in the building that is Dorich House and the collections within.

[i] *A Second Home* series. BBC/National Sound Archives, LP34712 Back 1. Broadcast 5/9/1972
[ii] Richard Hare wrote four books on Russian literature. His fifth book *The Art and Artists of Russia* (London: Methuen, 1965) was an illustrated survey of Russian Imperial Art and showcased much of his collection
[iii] *A Second Home* interview, op. cit.
[iv] Interview for the Tate Gallery archives. Ref: TAV 734A
[v] Ibid
[vi] The studio house is at 21 rue du Belvédère. It became a Listed Building in 1975 and is in an area of special architectural interest
[vii] Karla Britton *Auguste Perret* (London: Phaidon, 2001), pp. 107-8
[viii] Tate Gallery interview, op. cit
[ix] The correspondence can be found in the British Architectural Library. Ref: SaG/8/1
[x] For further information see Gretchen Liu *Pastel Portraits, Singapore's Architectural Heritage* (Singapore: Singapore Co-ordinating Committee, 1984)
[xi] Tate Gallery interview, op. cit.
[xii] Interview 10, Dorich House Archives
[xiii] A few sitters talk of taking medication or being ill during sittings, which was noted by Gordine, who declared she could not go on with the portrait until they were better as it would not be a true likeness
[xiv] Diary of Elizabeth Goold-Adams, the model for *Arise* (Dorich House collection 315).

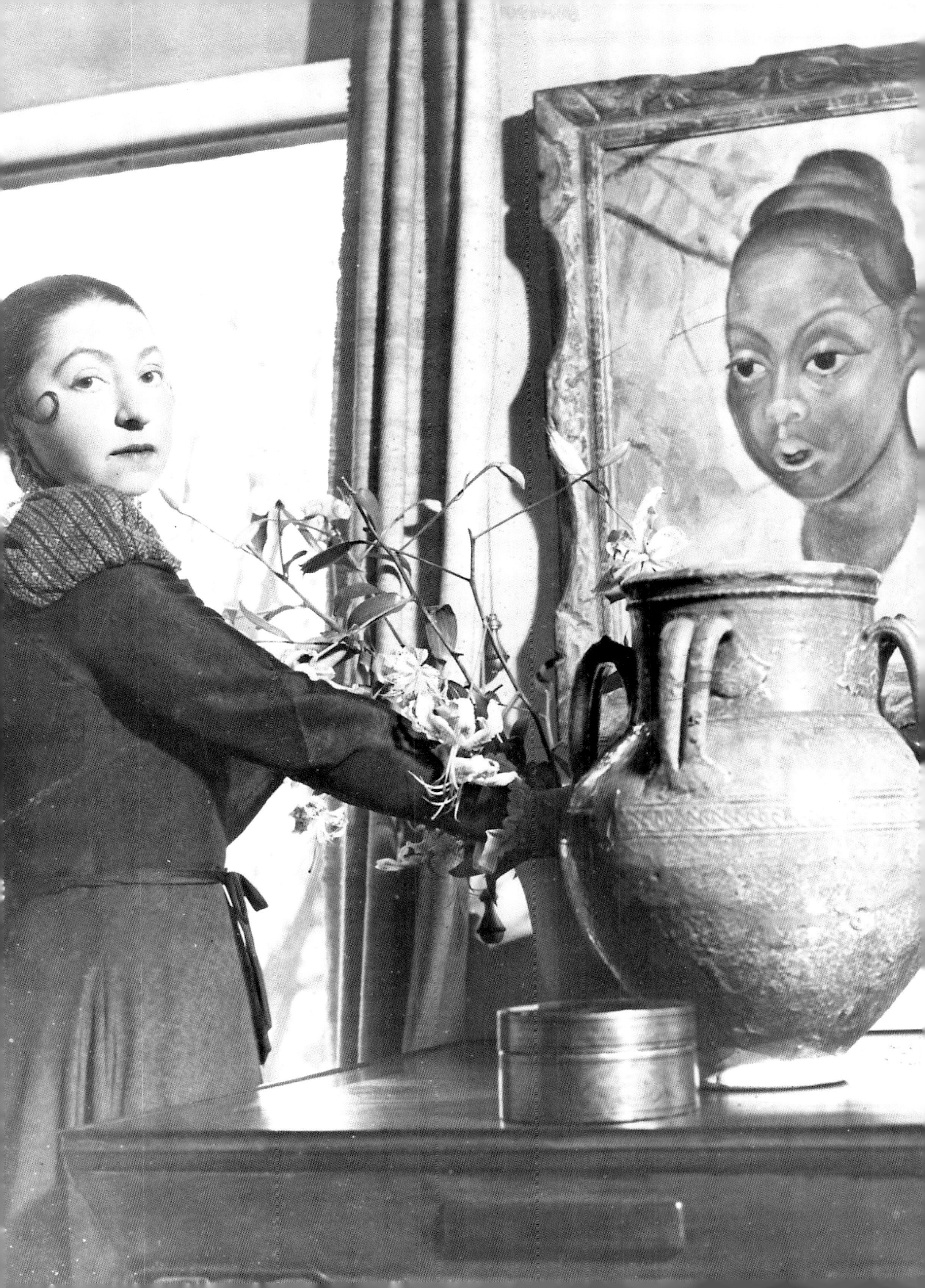

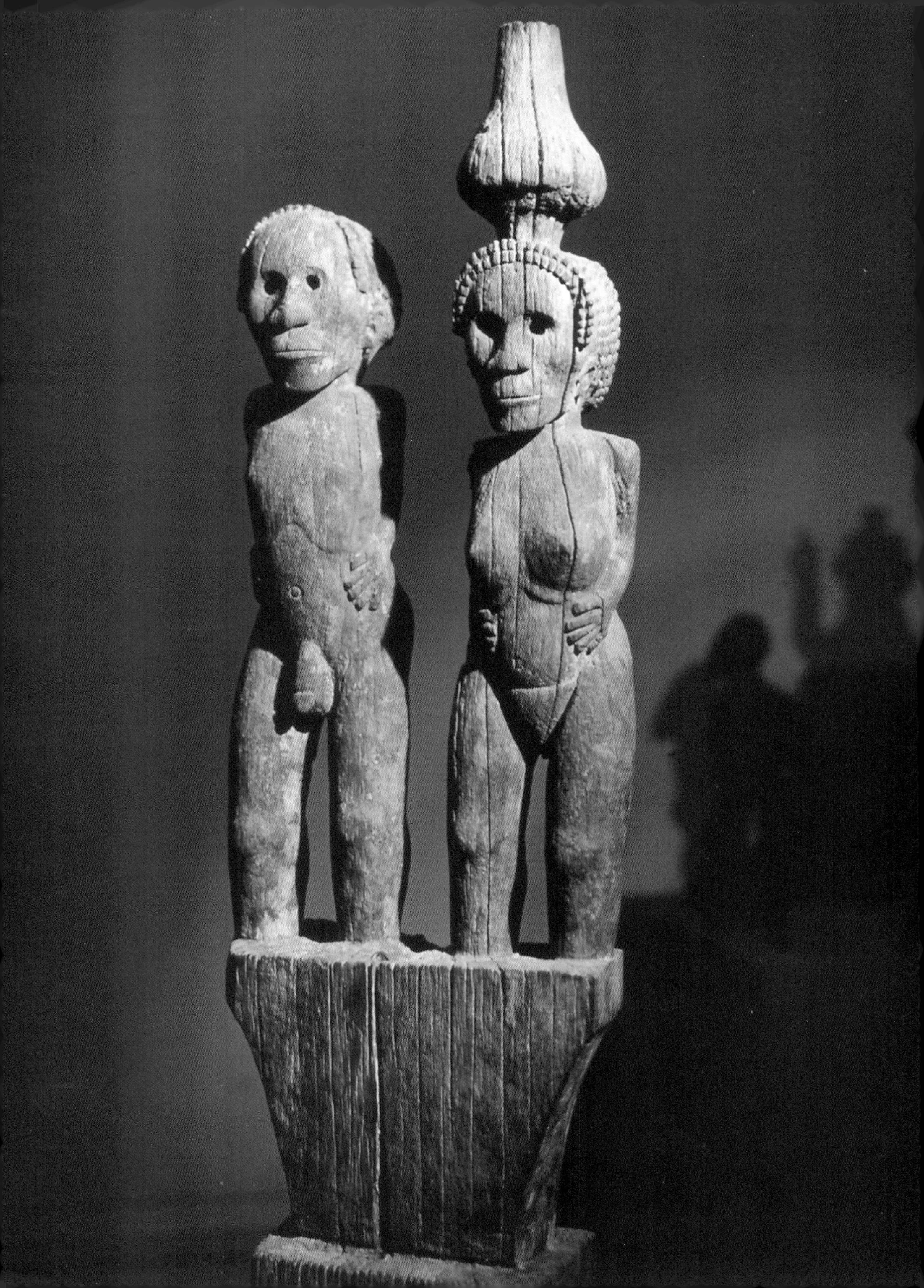

The Epstein Collection of Tribal Art

Geoffrey Ireland

I met Epstein in 1953 when he was offered the largest studio in the Sculpture Department at the Royal College of Art to carry out work too big for his own studio. At the same time I had been appointed as a tutor to introduce photography to the Graphic Design Department at the Royal College.

Epstein commissioned me to photograph the huge group *Social Consciousness*, which had just been cast in bronze, prior to shipping to Philadelphia. Epstein was so impressed by the photographs that he exclaimed, "Don't you leave me!" He placed these photographs on his bedroom mantlepiece where they stayed until his death in 1959.

These and subsequent photographs of Epstein's work over the following six years were published in my book *A Camera Study of the Sculptor at Work*, introduced by Laurie Lee and published by the Royal College of Art, and later by André Deutsch.

After Epstein's death I was commissioned by the Epstein Trust to photograph the tribal art collection. This proved to be an unforgettable experience.

At the age of five I was taken by the Town Astronomer 'to see the moon' through the telescope in the observatory at Williamson Park, Lancaster. Attached to the entrance of the observatory was a conservatory lit only by moonlight. Unexpectedly, passing through, half in and half out of shadows, I was faced with a large group of African sculptures, and what I felt in their presence proved more powerful than the moon.

Thirty-three years later I spent the night alone locked in a London gallery photographing the Epstein Collection. Here was more of what I met as a child, the same awe and mystery. So here in the dark, with my own moonlight, I hoped to share the experience through portraying these Art Magical Presences around me.

April 2005

left:
Fig. 21
Geoffrey Ireland
Architectural Carving
in the form of Male and Female figure, Madagascar
Formerly Jacob Epstein collection
Black and white photograph

overleaf:
Fig. 22
Geoffrey Ireland
Bedroom at Hyde Park Gate showing famous
Fang Head and Dogon Mother and Child, c.1959
Black and white photograph

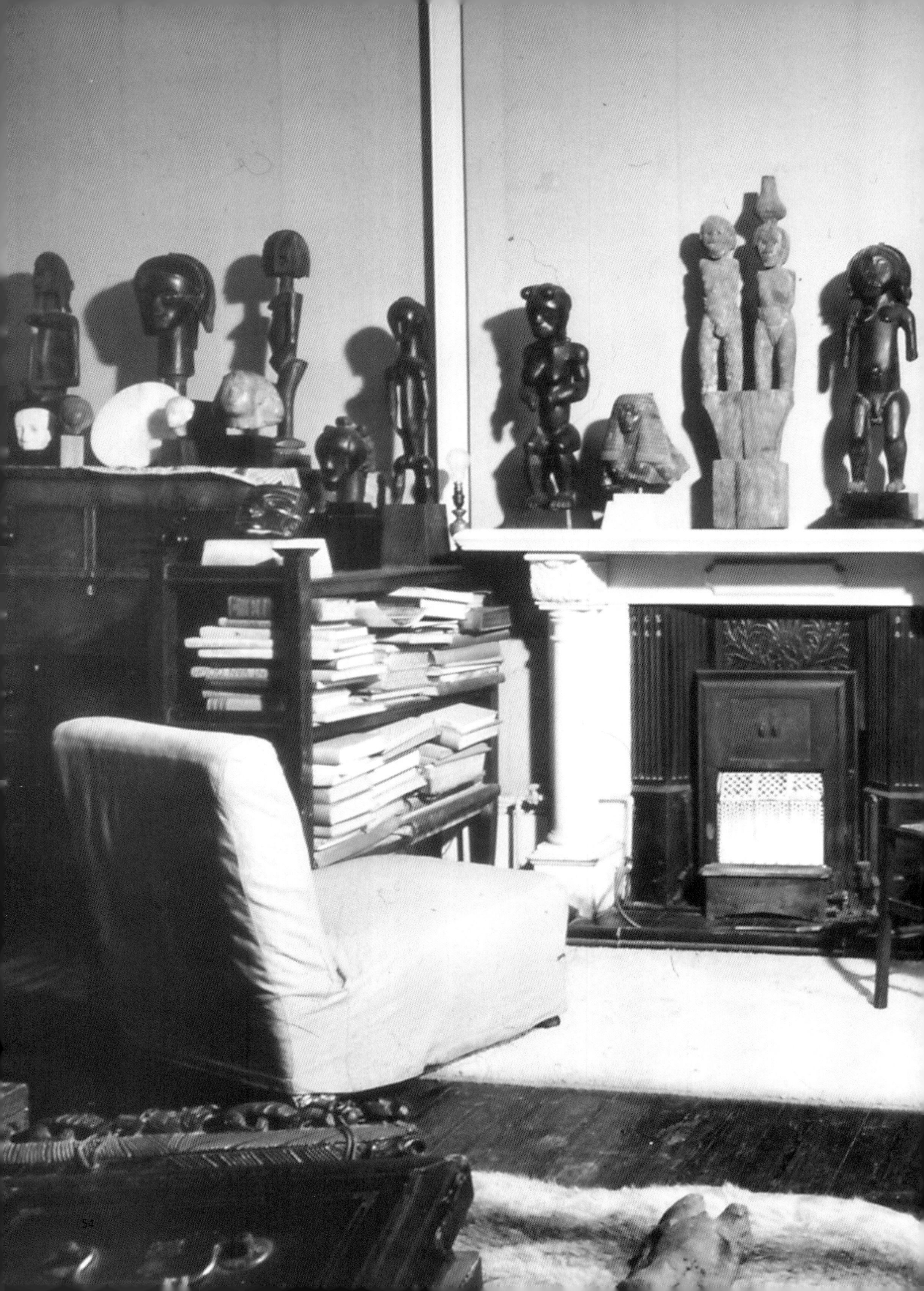

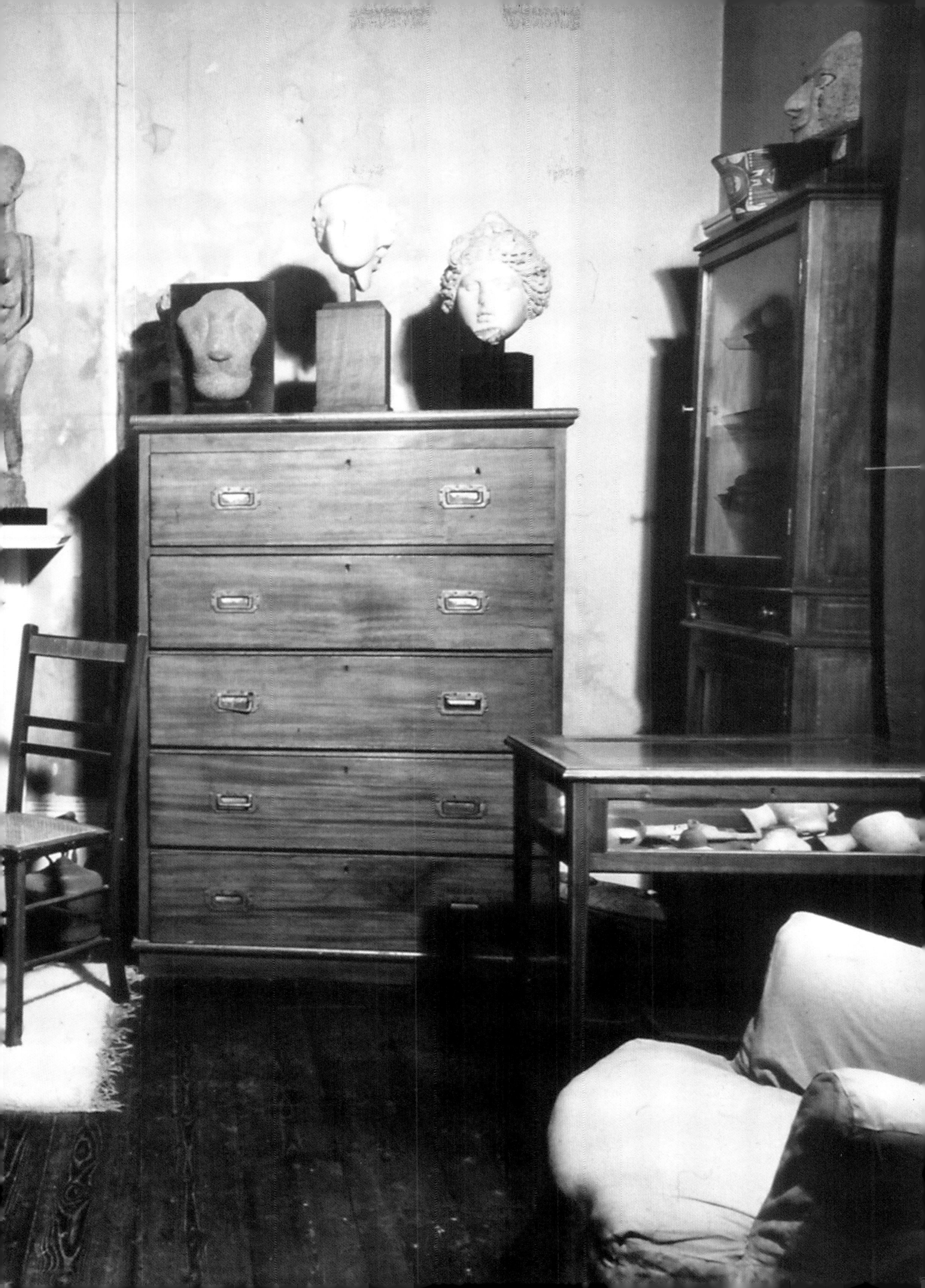

Dora

Dr Suzanne Ullman

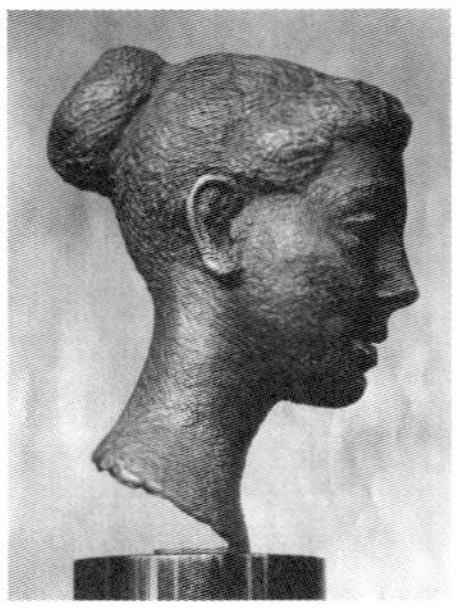

Fig. 23 Dora Gordine
Susanna, 1958

I first met Dora Gordine – the Honourable Mrs Hare – in 1956, when she accompanied her husband to our London home in Golders Green. Richard, her spouse, Professor of Slavonic Studies in the University of London, was writing a book on "The Art and Artists of Russia" and wanted to view my father's fine collection of figurines, made in the Gardner factory of pre-revolutionary Russia.

After a couple of visits a friendship developed, fuelled perhaps by a shared love of art and an interest in each other. We were intrigued and perhaps a little in awe of this unusual couple: Richard, so English, erudite and reserved; Dora, with her vivacious Russian temperament, exotic appearance and curl of hair plastered on to her cheeks on either side! Dora was fond of children and showed a lively interest in us – a family of five siblings, of Hungarian origin.

My father would invite the Hares to dinner or the theatre; and they would reciprocate by inviting us to their home, Dorich House, near Kingston. These visits were always memorable. The first challenge was locating Dorich House, hidden behind a wall and tall trees. After the bell was rung Dora would lean out of a second floor window, check on the visitors, a button would be pressed and the doors would open for us. Inside the foyer were housed dozens of slippers and we were required to exchange our outdoor shoes for a suitable pair – to save on housework! By this time Dora and Richard would have appeared to welcome us. Our gracious hosts led us through fine wrought iron gates, up the stairs to the large sculpture gallery on the right. We would sit there and talk over drinks, surrounded by Dora's numerous marvellous sculptures, before proceeding up a narrow flight of stairs to the private premises – comprising a bedroom, sitting room, dining room, bathroom and tiny kitchen. Everywhere we were surrounded by works of art – paintings, porcelain, figurines: it was the Hares avowed ambition to bequeath to the nation a museum of Russian art and they lived very frugally in order to achieve this aim.

Having prepared a good meal, Dora would preside over the beautifully laid table, while Richard acted as butler. After dinner the unique "Chinese moon" doors would be pulled aside and we would go into the adjoining sitting room for coffee. When my brother Louis was asked to play the violin, the sound of his music wafted up to us from the gallery below.

I was a 22-year old student when Dora and I first met and she promptly declared an interest in wanting to sculpt me. So it was that, in due course, I became a sitter and a more personal friendship developed between us, which lasted for the rest of her lifetime. Regrettably, due to my lack of availability, she was only able to complete my head. However, the time we spent together had a formative influence on me and I felt uniquely privileged, as a fledgling scientist, to have had an intimate peep into the world of an artist.

I would arrive in the morning and, after a good cup of coffee, the doors opposite the gallery would be opened and we would go into the studio – Dora's workplace. There were huge windows on one side and a revolving circular platform in the centre of the room, with a chair for me to sit on. All around the room were sculptures, in various states of completion.

Dora's method was to get to know her subject essentially – from the inside, as it were – before she embarked on work. She sat on a chair in front of me and, with the toe of her shoe, gently kicked the platform on which I was sitting, so that it revolved slowly and she could view me from every angle. And all the time we would talk – about everything under the sun.

I spent a day with Dora whenever I could and watched my head take shape in clay on the armature and then be wrapped in damp cloths at the end of the day. Richard worked in his office on the ground floor and only occasionally peeped around the door with a question. We usually had lunch together in the kitchen. Dora had taught herself to cook after her marriage and excelled at it. "At first I burned everything and just had to fling it out of the window" she would reminisce, in her inimitable style. She was always ready to learn and, though she lived for her art, humanity took precedence. "First be a woman and then a professional," she would urge.

After my portrait head was exhibited in the sixth annual exhibition of the Society of Portrait Sculptors in 1958[i] (I was asked by Dora not to go there – I know not why, but I respected her wishes) I bought it and

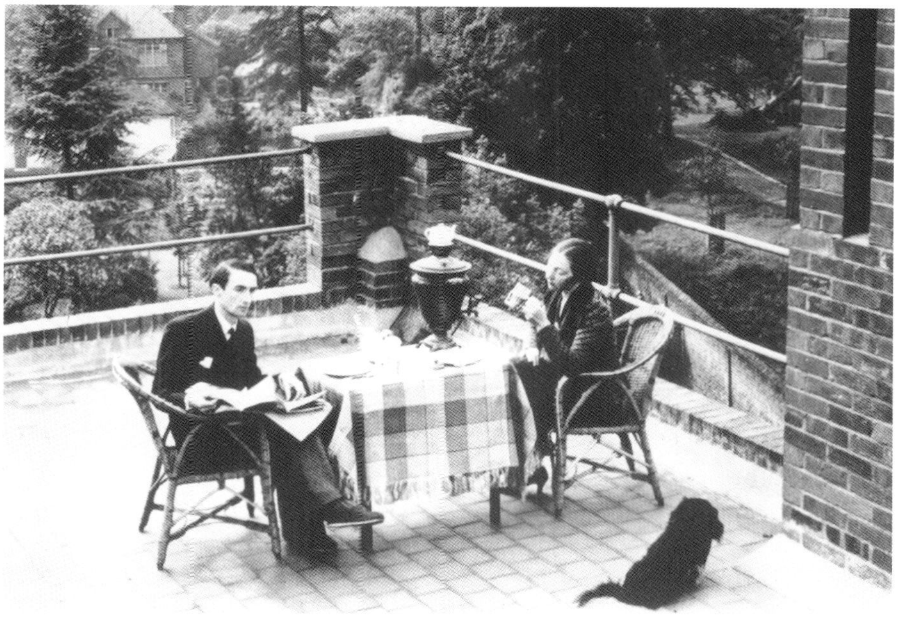

Fig. 24 *Dora Gordine and Richard Hare having tea on the roof terrace at Dorich House*, c.1948

presented it to my parents for their silver wedding anniversary. My face in bronze looks quite asymmetrical: one profile is smiling, the other looks sad. I felt she caught the essence of me.

In 1961 I moved to Edinburgh, where news reached me of Richard's sudden and premature death in 1966. Dora never really recovered from her devastating loss, though she struggled on valiantly. By this time my family had rather tenuous links with her, finding her dominant personality difficult to cope with. I, however, visited her every time I was in London. We would go shopping or sit in the kitchen or the overgrown, romantic garden, sewing, knitting, talking. Cooking, medical matters, fairy tales and her Asian experiences were among the many topics discussed. When I stayed overnight, I slept in the studio with her sculptures all around me – an unforgettable experience.

Dora was a complex and engaging personality: opinionated, exacting, superstitious (she once refused a gift of knives from my father "lest it cut the friendship"), charming, funny, generous and of great integrity – though somewhat prone to exaggeration! She would never prostitute her art for gain. She had a wicked sense of humour and loved poking fun at pomposity. She would buy some cheap material in Chelsea, design and make a fantastic dress and wear it to a garden party. When asked which Paris fashion house she ordered her garment from, she would spin a story shamelessly – and have a good laugh about it afterwards.

Dora's shopping habits were idiosyncratic. She returned from Asia on a cargo boat, bringing oriental furniture with her; from California she returned with a large cooker; and from Spain she brought back a balcony (!) – which was then integrated into Dorich House. She would buy coffee by the sack – all to Richard's silent amazement.When Richard died Dora locked their bedroom, took up residence in the sitting room and slept on the sofa. Some nineteen years later she invited me over, opened the bedroom and asked me to help clear it. It was like entering the tomb of a pharaoh – I felt I was on hallowed ground. Alas, the ground heaved under our feet with the maggots which had taken up residence in the carpet in the intervening years.

Dora was an insomniac and one night in the 1980s thieves broke into Dorich House at night. They shone a torch in her eyes and set about removing valuables and cutting paintings from their frames. It must have been a terrifying experience. Subsequently she had bars put on her windows.

In Dora's latter years it became a ritual that we spend New Year's Day together. I would bring my honey (to sweeten the year ahead) and a round sweet-and-sour loaf from Scotland – gestures which had a special symbolism for her. We were about to celebrate together again, when Dora suddenly passed away on 29 December, 1991. She enriched my life in many ways and continues to do so for, as a collector, I am fortunate to have her creations around me. "My sculptures are my children," she used to say and it is through these 'children' that she continues to live.

Glasgow, November 2005

i The sculpture was exhibit no. 75 and was entitled *Susanna*

Sitting for Epstein

An Interview with Betty Peterson

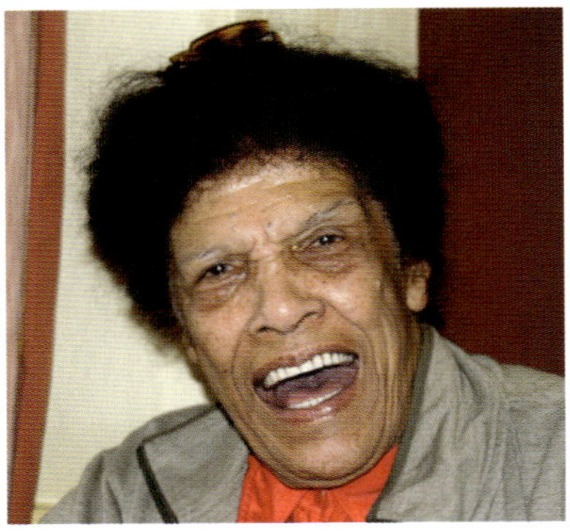

Mrs Betty Peterson (formerly Peters), one of Epstein's most striking black-British models from the 1940s, talked to co-curators Sarah MacDougall and Rachel Dickson about sitting for Epstein.

Born on 28 November 1919 in Pontypridd, Wales, Betty was one of seven surviving children born to an Irish Catholic mother and black Ethiopian, possibly Falasha, father believed to be of Jewish descent.[i] Her mother finding it difficult to cope, Betty along with her sister Kathleen (known as Kay)[ii] and a brother, was brought up in a local orphanage; their mother was killed in an accident at Hyde Park Corner in 1925.

Betty moved to Whitechapel in London's East End, to take up domestic work when she was about 17, living at 33 Amberson Street. She vividly recalled her Jewish neighbours, particularly remembering their warmth and friendliness towards her. Her conversation is still incongruously peppered with Yiddish phrases, pronounced with the traces of a soft Welsh accent, recalling the names of the important Jewish Festivals and, with particular fondness, traditional Jewish dishes such as *lockschen*, and chicken soup with *kneidlach,* which she regularly ate.

However, her modelling career with Epstein, which came about after a chance meeting in Shaftesbury Avenue, did not begin until several years later. Although she had read about him in the press, Betty did not recognise the famous sculptor. But something about this ill-matched couple: the short, stocky, red-haired Epstein, and his tall, thin and striking companion who seemed to tower over him (Kathleen Garman, the woman who would become his second wife), caught her eye and she laughed, attracting Epstein's attention. As soon as he caught sight of her, he immediately turned and asked, with a slight American twang, if she was a model. "No," replied Betty, at which Epstein rejoined, "Do you want to be one?", and he gave her his card requesting that she come to 18 Hyde Park Gate for a sitting. "I'll try anything once!" Betty replied, but in fact she did not take up the offer until they had had two further chance encounters outside the Ivy restaurant in West Street, when Epstein repeated his earlier invitation.

For her first sitting Betty took along her sister Kay to act as chaperone, but Epstein soon made her feel comfortable and afterwards she always went alone. She was made very welcome by the artist and his first wife, Margaret and vividly recalls how they always drank tea together at a scrubbed oak table in the front room. Many other models and visitors came and went (some famous, like Churchill, who had a house opposite Epstein's; or the well-known pianist Maria Donska; some less so, like the girl who looked after Epstein's children and posed for the sculpture *The Mexican Girl)*. Elsewhere in the house she noted his vast collection of ethnographic figures, which seemed to her rather scary at the time. Altogether Betty sat regularly for a period of about two years, going for an hour or so at a time, for which she received "about £1" a sitting (delivered under the table by Epstein, who seemed rather shy over money). Her relations with the whole family were friendly and she recalled once taking Epstein's grandchildren to the Tivoli picture house to see a film. She enjoyed Epstein's company and found him

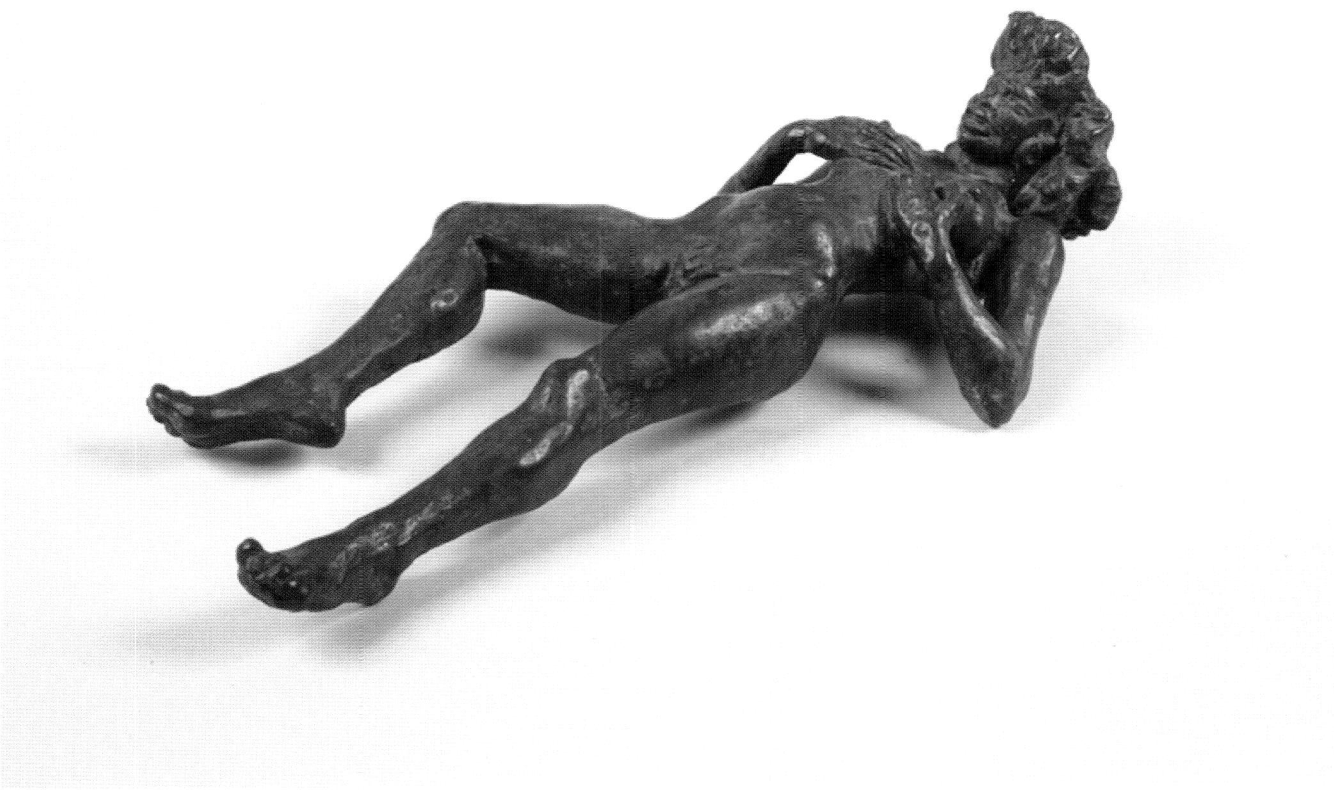

27 Jacob Epstein
Nude Study D (Betty Peters), 1943-5

considerate; their sessions only finally came to an end when the demands of family life made it impossible for Betty to carry on sitting.iii

Betty remembers sitting for about thirteen figures in all – mainly recumbent – particularly recalling one piece where she posed with a ball. Mostly, Epstein allowed her to settle into a pose, only occasionally asking her to assume a particular one, while he observed her and applied clay to a wooden armature. Of these, six recumbent nudes (all 1943-5) and a fine over-life-size bust (dated 1939, though Betty believes they did not meet until c. 1943)iv have been positively identified and catalogued in Dr Evelyn Silber's *The Sculpture of Epstein: with a complete catalogue*.v

Even today, at 86, Betty retains the striking looks, elegant carriage and fascinating personality that first caught Epstein's attention more than sixty years ago, and provided the inspiration for another series of important works as part of the sculptor's ongoing quest to 'embrace the exotic'.

i Many of her elder brothers and sisters died before she was born, but Betty believes that her mother gave birth to up to 17 children in all
ii Another sister, Rachel, is believed to have modelled for Augustus John
iii She had a daughter, three step-children and three nephews to look after
iv Although she cannot be certain about the date, she believes it was in the early 1940s as it was after her marriage c. 1938-9, the birth of her daughter in 1940 and her husband's departure to join the war
v The number of sculptures is seven, cited E Silber: *The Sculpture of Epstein* with a complete catalogue (Oxford: Phaidon Press, 1986), p.187: cat no. (307) *Betty Peters*, 1939, bronze, h 68.5; p.193: (341) *Nude Study A* (Betty Peters), 1943-5, bronze, l 72.4; (342) *Nude Study B* (Betty Peters), 1943-5, bronze, l 58.4; (343) *Nude Study C* (Betty Peters), 1943-5, bronze; (344) *Nude Study D* (Betty Peters), 1943-5, bronze, l 34; p.194: (349) *Nude Study* (Betty Peters), bronze; and (351) *Nude Study* (Betty Peters), bronze, l 50

Compiled from conversations with the curators,
South London, 11 November 2005

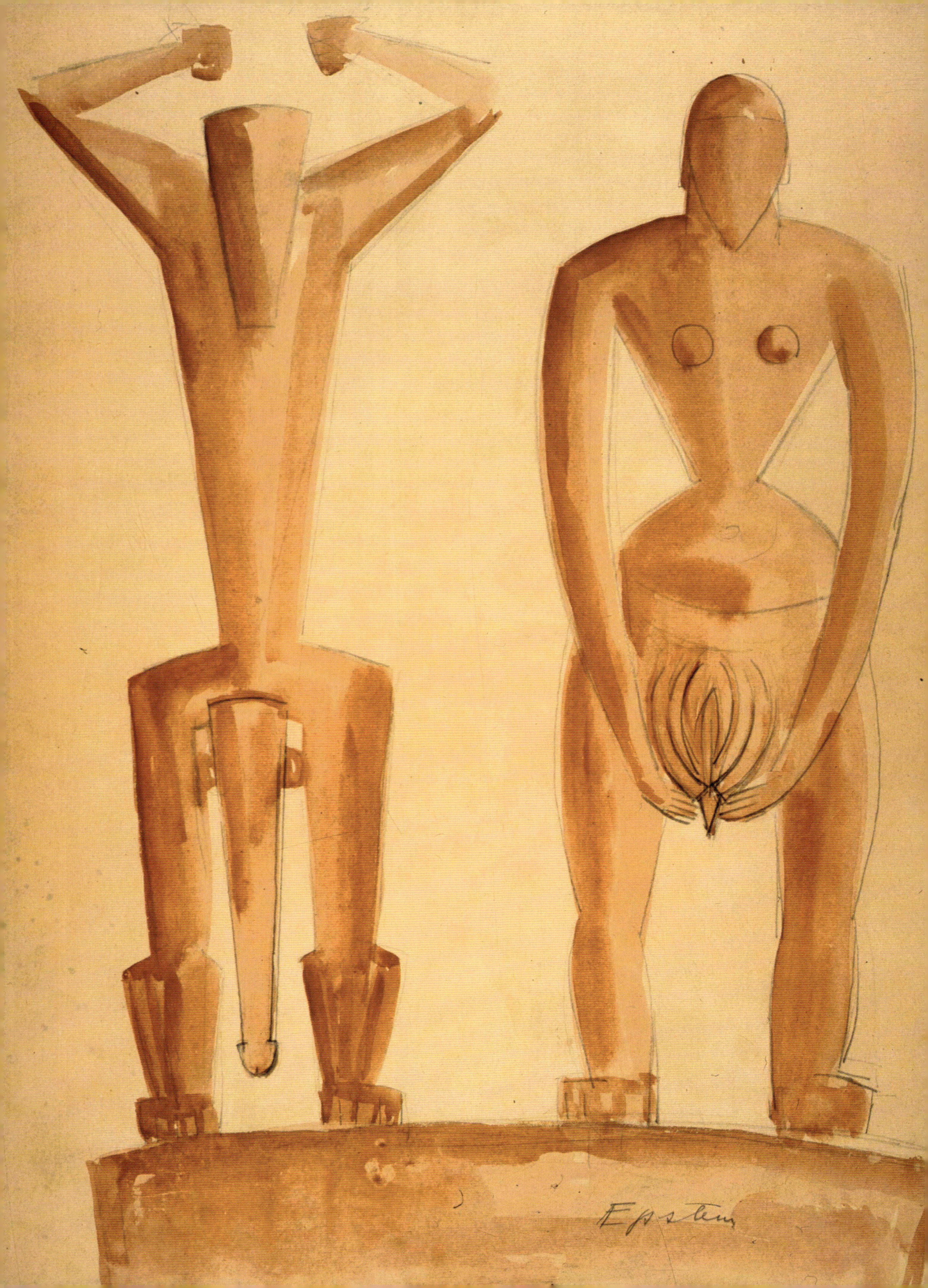
Epstein

Catalogue of Works

11 Jacob Epstein
Study for Man-Woman, 1913

Dimensions are given in cms, height before width

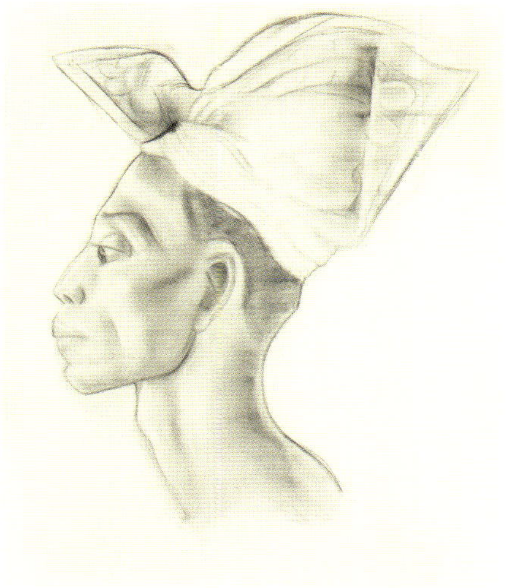

36 Dora Gordine
Malay Head, 1930-35

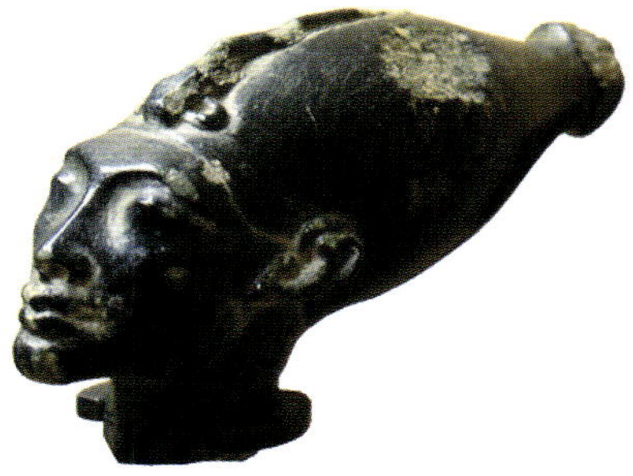

48 ***Head of Akhenaton***
(Egyptian), c.1450 BC

Works by Sir Jacob Epstein

1
Self-Portrait
1901
Red chalk on paper
29.5 x 22.5
Garman Ryan Collection,
The New Art Gallery Walsall

2
Head of Nan
1909
Pencil on paper
48 x 33.5
Garman Ryan Collection,
The New Art Gallery Walsall

3
Portrait Head of a Young Girl
c.1909
Pencil on paper
49.53 x 36.83
Private Collection

4
Sun Goddess, Crouching
1909-10
Limestone
h 37.5
Courtesy Nottingham City Museums
and Galleries: Nottingham Castle

5
Study for Tomb of Oscar Wilde
Inscribed 'In Memory of Oscar Wilde'
c.1909-11
Pencil on paper
49 x 60
Garman Ryan Collection,
The New Art Gallery Walsall

6
Rom
Inscribed 'ROM'
1910
Stone
87.5 x 59.5 x 57.7
National Museums and Galleries
of Wales

7
Study for Figure of Maternity
c.1910
Pencil on paper
69.7 x 55.9
Leeds Museums & Galleries
(City Art Gallery)

8
One of the Hundred Pillars of the
Secret Temple
Inscribed 'One of the Hundred Pillars
of the Secret Temple'
c.1910
Pencil on paper
36.75 x 25.4
Private Collection, courtesy of James
Hyman Fine Art, London

9
Nan the Dreamer
1911
Bronze
28 x 35.5
Garman Ryan Collection,
The New Art Gallery Walsall

10
Nan (The Dreamer) – head and
shoulders
1911
Bronze
h 14
Victor and Gretha Arwas, London

right:
50 *Hei-Tiki* (New-Zealand, Maori)

far right:
Fig. 25 Jacob Epstein
Drawing XVI from Blast No. 1: Review of the Great English Vortex
1914

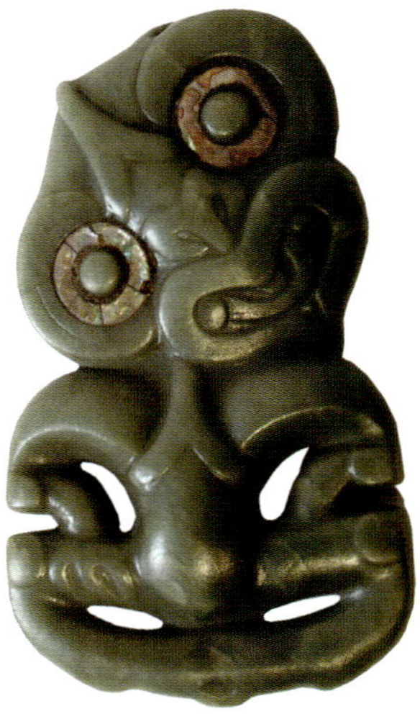

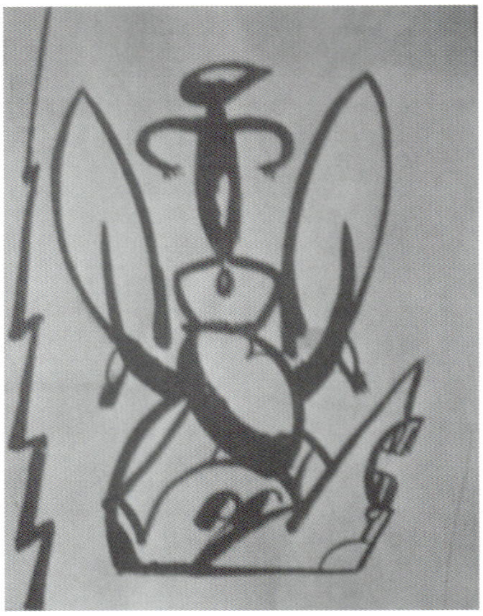

11
Study for Man-Woman
Signed (br) 'Epstein'
1913
Graphite and orange wash on orange-brown paper
56.1 x 41.3
The British Museum, London
(London only)

12
Study for Birth
c.1913
Pencil on paper
62 x 52
Ivor Braka Ltd, London

13
Study for the Rock Drill
c.1913
Charcoal on paper
67.7 x 42.5
Garman Ryan Collection,
The New Art Gallery Walsall

14
Third Portrait of Meum (Mask)
1918
Bronze
h 28
Victor and Gretha Arwas, London

15
Seated Figure Study for Rima
1923-25
Pencil and wash on paper
47 x 59.7
Leeds Museums and Galleries
(City Art Gallery)

16
Head Study for Rima
1923-25
Pencil and coloured wash on paper
47 x 59.7
Leeds Museums and Galleries
(City Art Gallery)

17
The Little Negress
Signed (bl) 'Epstein'
1928
Pencil on paper
47.6 x 55.9
Tate. Purchased 1928

18
Negress
Signed (br) 'Epstein'
1928
Pencil on paper
45.7 x 55.9
Tate. Purchased 1928

19
Genesis II
Signed (lr) 'Epstein'
1929-30
Pencil on paper
26.5 x 17.5
Private Collection, London

20
Sunita
c.1930
Watercolour on paper
44 x 58
Garman Ryan Collection,
The New Art Gallery Walsall

21
And the Spirit of God moved upon the Face of the Waters
1930-32
Pencil and watercolour on paper
58 x 45
Birmingham Museum and Art Galleries

22
Second Portrait of Lydia
1931
Bronze
48.5 x 43 x 32
Ben Uri Gallery, The London Jewish Museum of Art

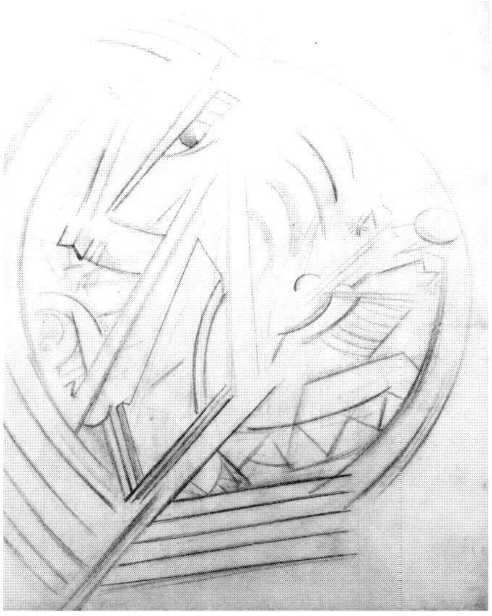

12 Jacob Epstein
Study for Birth, c.1913

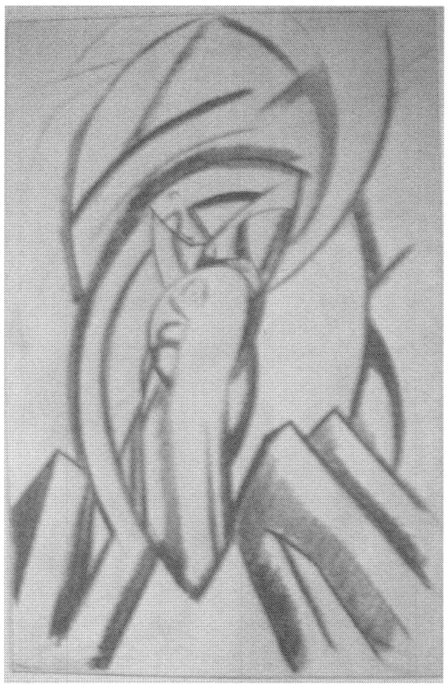

Fig. 26 Jacob Epstein
Drawing XV from Blast No. 1: Review of the Great English Vortex 1914

23
Indian Mother and Child
Signed (bl) 'Epstein'
c.1932
Pencil on paper
49 x 56
Garman Ryan Collection,
The New Art Gallery Walsall

24
Rani Rama
1934
Bronze
h 57.2
Victor and Gretha Arwas, London

25
Shulamite Woman (Arab Girl)
1935
Bronze
h 52.5
Ben Uri Gallery,
The London Jewish Museum of Art

26
Illustration for Fleurs du Mal
signed (br) 'Epstein'
1938
pencil on paper
60 x 47
Victor and Gretha Arwas, London

27
Nude Study D (Betty Peters)
1943-5
Bronze
l 34
Victor and Gretha Arwas, London

Works by Dora Gordine

28
Guadeloupe Head / Negress
Signed 'Dora Gordine 8/8' and
'VALSUANI CIRE PERDUE BRONZE'
1928
Bronze
36 x 23 x 23
Tate. Transferred from the
Victoria & Albert Museum 1983

29
Chinese Head / Chinaman / Chinese Philosopher
Signed 'Dora Gordine Paris'
1926
Bronze with wood base (Valsuani cast)
46.7 x 22.3 x 22
Dorich House Museum,
Kingston University

30
Javanese Dancer
Signed 'Dora Gordine'
1927
Bronze with wood base (Valsuani cast)
143.2 x 65.1 x 37
Dorich House Museum,
Kingston University

31
Baby's Head
Signed 'Dora Gordine, Paris 4/8'
1928
Bronze with wood base (Valsuani cast)
31.9 x 16.2 x 19.6
Dorich House Museum,
Kingston University

32
Mongolian Head
Signed 'Dora Gordine 1928'
1928
Bronze (Valsuani cast)
49 x 21 x 26
Tate. Presented anonymously
through the National Art Collections
Fund 1928

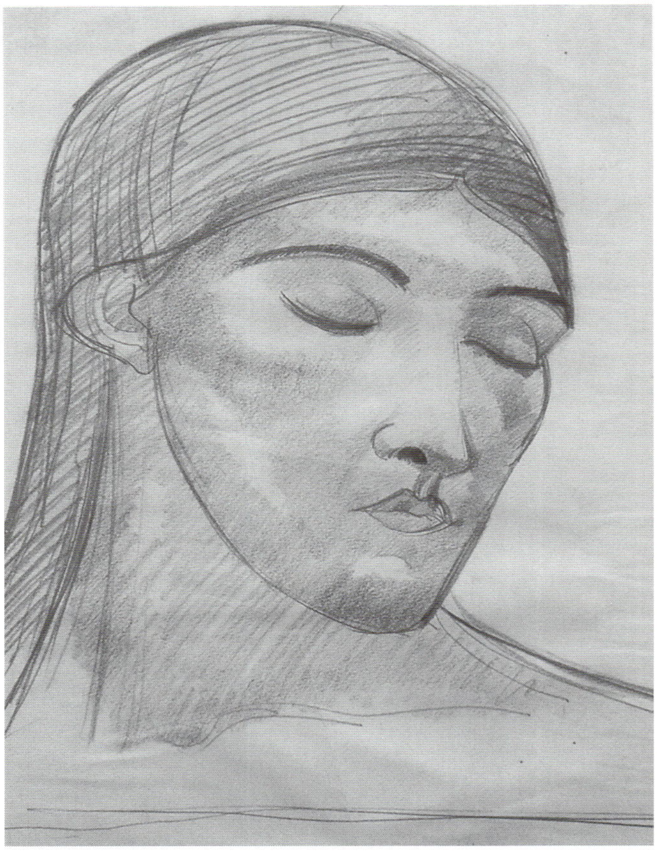

2 Jacob Epstein
Head of Nan, 1909 (detail)

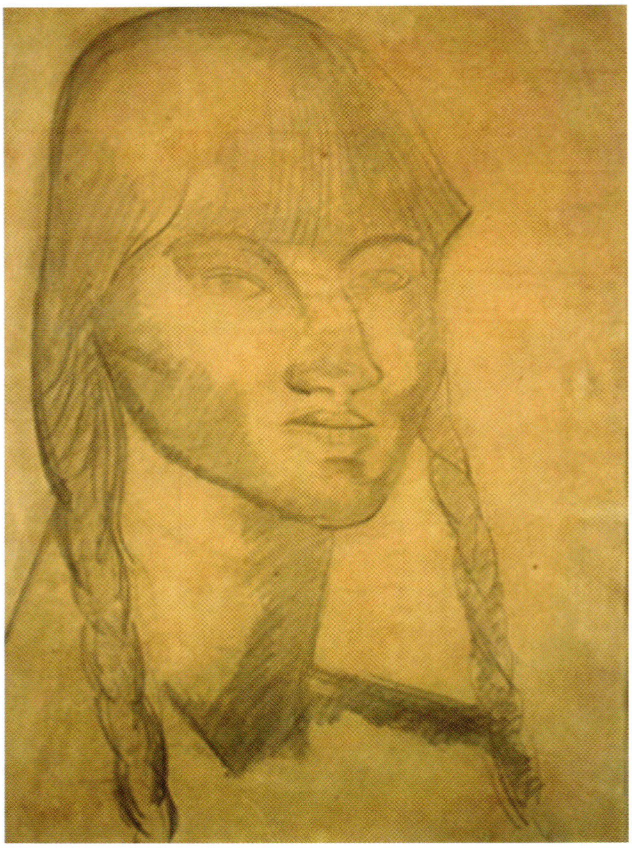

3 Jacob Epstein
Portrait of a Young Girl, c.1909 (detail)

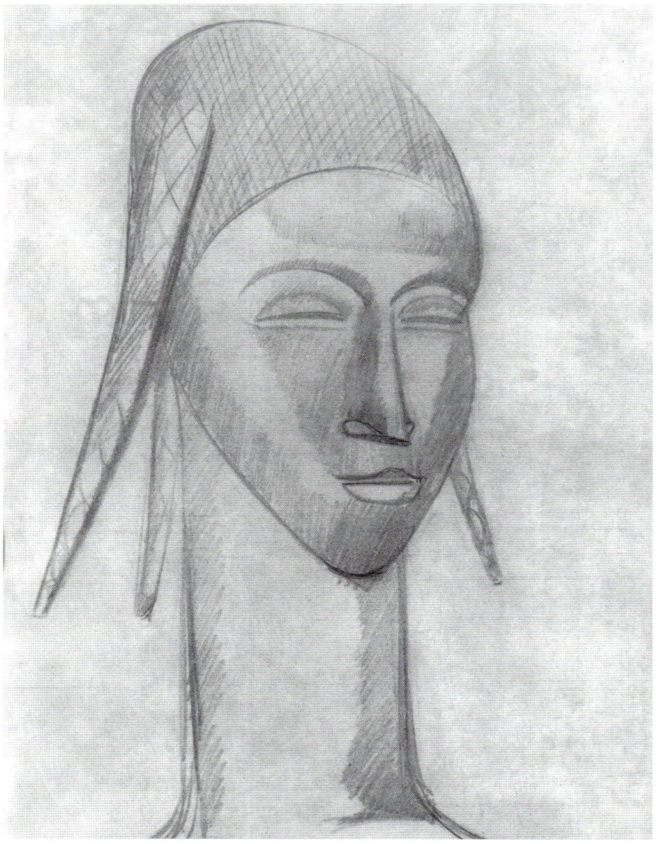

Fig. 27 Jacob Epstein
Portrait of Nan Condron as the Brummer Head, c.1913 (detail)

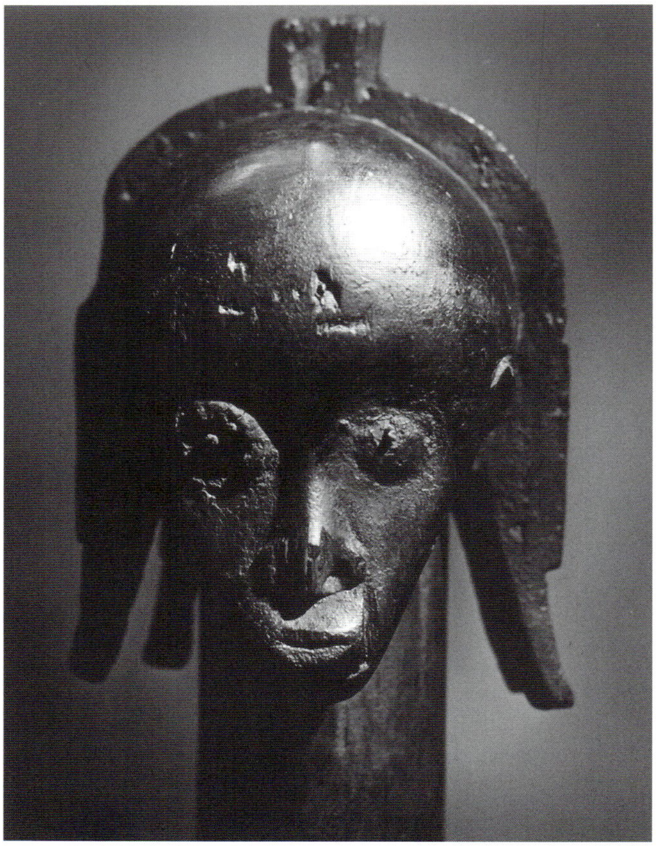

Fig. 28 Geoffrey Ireland
Reliquary Head, Fang – Gabon (The Brummer Head)

33
African Head
Signed 'Dora Gordine 3/4'
1929
Bronze with wood base (Valsuani cast)
41.2 x 13.8 x 26.5 with mount
Dorich House Museum,
Kingston University

34
Mask of a Greek Boy
Signed 'Dora Gordine 3/4'
1929
Bronze with wood base
29.4 x 19.9 x 20.6
Dorich House Museum,
Kingston University

35
Javanese Head
Signed 'Dora Gordine 1/8'
1931
Bronze
45.8 x 21 x 27.5
Tate. Presented by the
Hon. Richard Hare 1933

36
Malay Head
1930-35
Black crayon and pastel on paper
66 x 56
Dorich House Museum,
Kingston University

37
Two Women with Earrings
1930-35
Black crayon and pastel on paper
66 x 56
Dorich House Museum,
Kingston University

38
Two Temple Dancers
1930-35
Black crayon and pastel on paper
66 x 56
Dorich House Museum,
Kingston University

39
Standing Nude
1930-35
Black crayon and pastel on paper
66 x 56
Dorich House Museum,
Kingston University

40
Study for Pagan I
c.1933
Black crayon and pastel on paper
66 x 56
Dorich House Museum,
Kingston University

41
Study for Pagan II
c.1933
Black crayon and pastel on paper
66 x 56
Dorich House Museum,
Kingston University

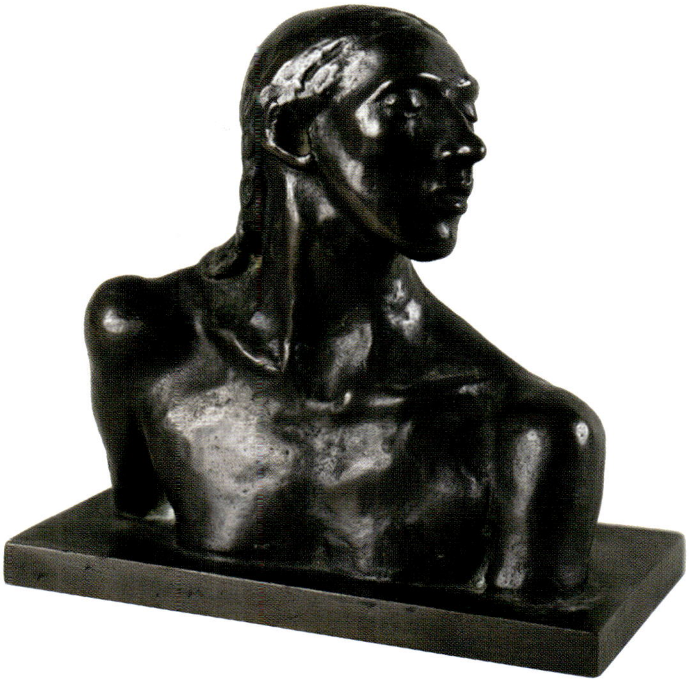

10 Jacob Epstein
Nan (The Dreamer), 1911

below left:
39 Dora Gordine
Standing Nude, 1930-35

below right:
7 Jacob Epstein
Study for Figure of Maternity, c.1910

45 Dora Gordine
Flawless Crystal, 1949

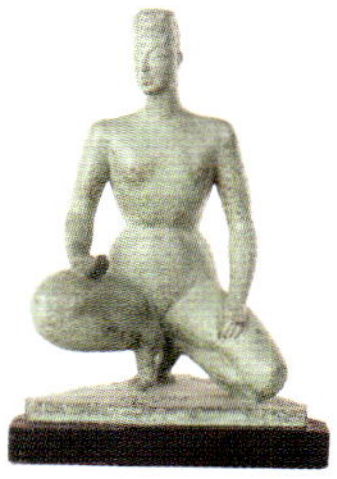

38 Dora Gordine
Two Temple Dancers, 1930-35

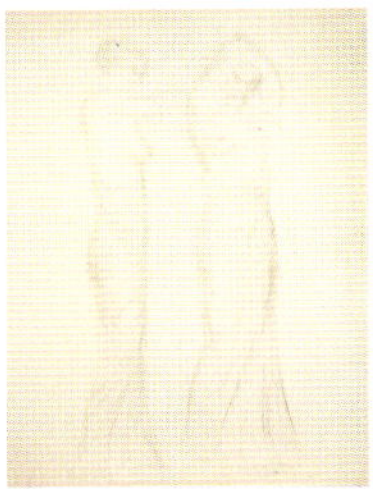

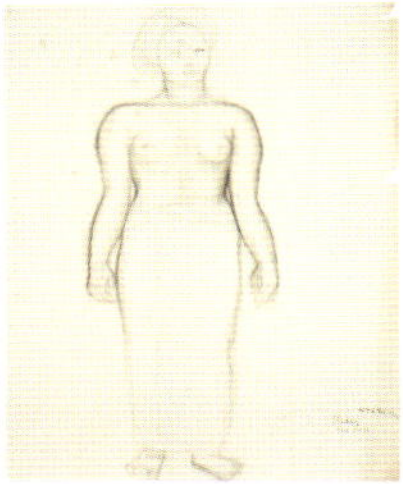

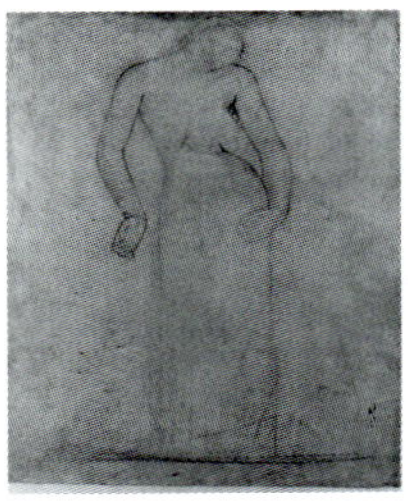

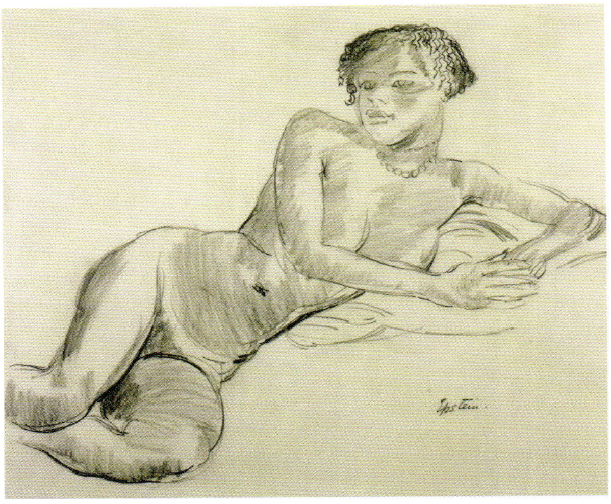

18 Jacob Epstein
Negress,
1928

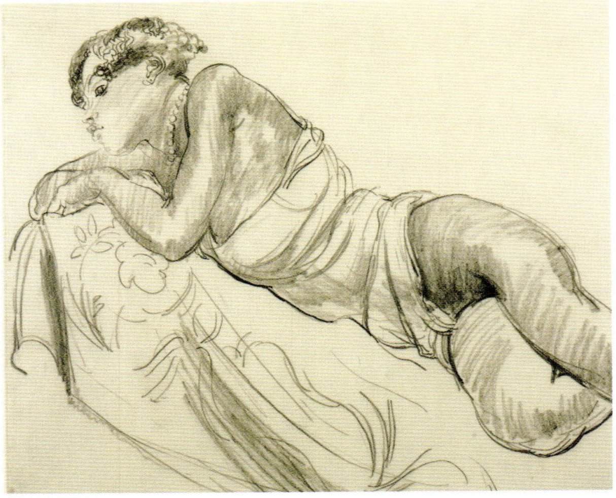

17 Jacob Epstein
The Little Negress,
1928

42
Two Oriental Girls
1930-35
Black crayon and pastel on paper
66 x 56
Dorich House Museum,
Kingston University

43
Seated Oriental Woman with Arms Raised
1930-35
Black crayon and pastel on paper
66 x 56
Dorich House Museum,
Kingston University

44
A Malay Sultana (The Tungku Ampuan of Jahore)
Signed 'Dora Gordine 1/8'
1932
Bronze
35 x 22.2 x 33.6
Tate. Bequeathed by Mrs. Rhoda Symons 1937

45
Flawless Crystal
Signed 'Dora Gordine 5/6'
1949
Bronze with onyx base
(Morris Singer cast)
38.5 x 25.4 x 23.8
Dorich House Museum,
Kingston University

46
Black Orchid
Signed 'Dora Gordine 3/4'
Bronze
43.6 x 15 x 18
Dorich House Museum,
Kingston University

Ethnographic Works

47
Mask of Nefertiti (Egyptian)
1350-1300 BC
Plaster
h 17
Garman Ryan Collection,
The New Art Gallery Walsall

48
Head of Akhenaton (Egyptian)
c.1450BC
Stone
h 11
Garman Ryan Collection,
The New Art Gallery Walsall

49
Head of a Bodhisattva (Longmen, Henan Province, China)
c. 6-7th century
Limestone
h 13.5
Garman Ryan Collection,
The New Art Gallery Walsall

50
Hei-Tiki (New Zealand, Maori)
Greenstone and mother of pearl
h 12.5
Garman Ryan Collection,
The New Art Gallery Walsall

Ephemera

51
Jacob Epstein, with a foreword by Hubert Wellington
Seventy-five Drawings
London: J. Saville & Co., 1929
Victor and Gretha Arwas, London

52
Ed. Wyndham Lewis
Blast No. 1:
Review of the Great English Vortex
Santa Barbara, California: Black Sparrow Press, 1981
Facsimile
Private Collection, London

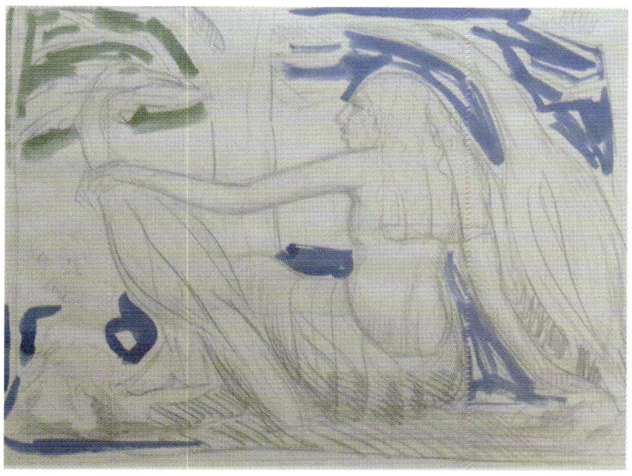

15 Jacob Epstein
Seated Figure Study for Rima,
1923-25

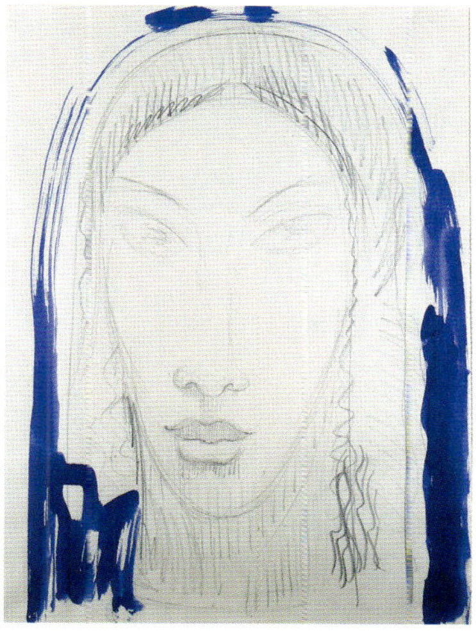

16 Jacob Epstein
Head Study for Rima,
1923-25

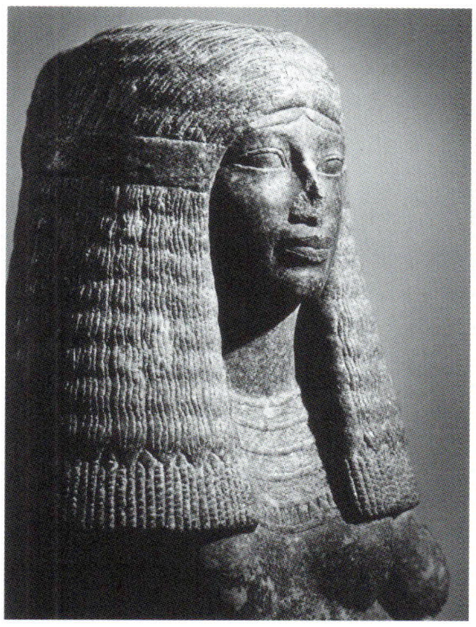

Fig. 29 Geoffrey Ireland
Head of Lady in Heavy Wig, Egyptian 18th Dynasty

Fig. 30 Jacob Epstein
Rima (Memorial to W H Hudson), 1923-25 (detail)

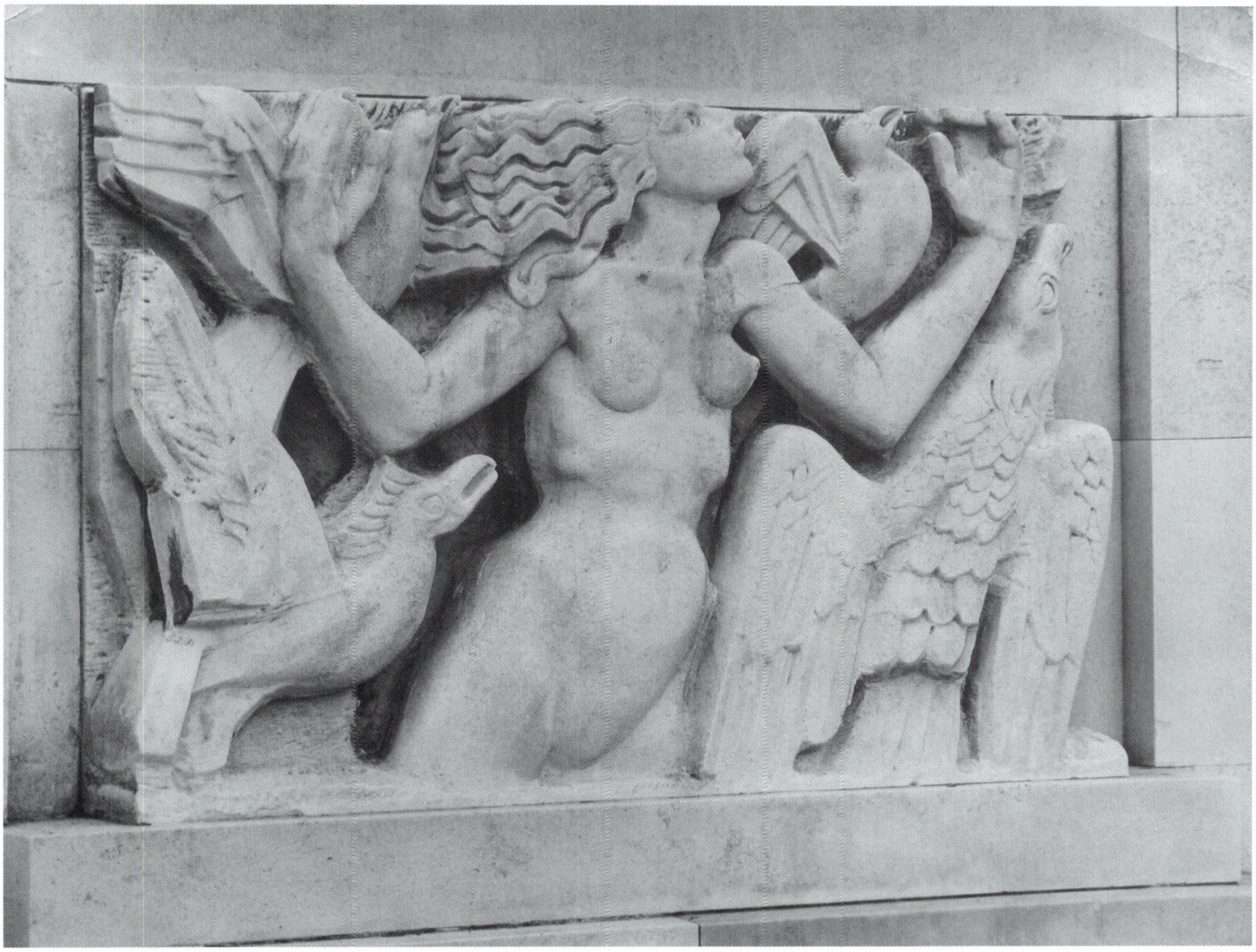

Chronology

Jacob Epstein Abbreviated Chronology:

We are grateful to Dr Evelyn Silber for assistance with this chronology, abbreviated from *Jacob Epstein Sculpture and Drawings* (Leeds: W S Maney and Son, in association with The Henry Moore Centre for the Study of Sculpture, 1989)

10 November 1880 born at 102 Hester Street, New York, the third child of Max and Mary Solomon Epstein, Jewish-Polish immigrants

1886 Contracts pleurisy and is ill for several years

c.1891 Wins a Cooper Union art competition

1893 Attends PS Seven and the East Side Settlement; registers at the Art Students' League

1894 Studies at the Art Students' League (until 1902)

1896 Attends James Kirk Paulding's classes at the community Guild, where he is introduced to the writings of Conrad, Ruskin, Turgenev and Whitman

1898 Organises an exhibition of work by local artists at the Hebrew Institute, New York. Spends the winter with the painter, Bernard Gussow, on Greenwood Lake, New Jersey, where he decides to be a sculptor

1899 Remains in rented rooms overlooking Hester Street after his family moves to 1661 Madison Avenue; employed as physical education instructor and tenement inspector; begins to sell his drawings

1900 Employed in a New York bronze foundry, draws Lower East Side life, illustrates Hitchins Hapgood's *Four Poets of the Ghetto* and *The Foreign Stage in New York*. Turns down an offer to work with Thomas Eakins in Philadelphia

1901 Attends Barnard's modelling classes at the Art Students' League (1901-2) and receives the commission to illustrate Hapgood's *The Spirit of the Ghetto*

1902 *The Spirit of the Ghetto* is published; first studio burns down; issued with a passport and arrives in Paris on 3-4 October to witness anti-Semitic demonstrations attending Zola's funeral. Shares a studio with Gussow, attends modelling atelier at the Ecole des Beaux-Arts, visits Louvre, Musée Guimet (Indian and Far Eastern art), Musée Cernuschi (Chinese Art) and a 'mass of primitive sculpture' at the Trocadero. Probably begins the drawings for Whitman's *Calamus*

1903 Studies for eighteen months under Jean Paul Laurens at the Académie Julian; visits Rodin; meets Margaret 'Peggy' Dunlop and makes a brief visit to Florence

1904 Lives at 5 rue Campagne Première, Montparnasse; models or carves his first sculptures; visits England and the British Museum

1905 Destroys the contents of Paris studio; moves to London with Peggy Dunlop; has reference from Rodin. Lives and works at 219 Stanhope Street, St Pancras; introduced to George Bernard Shaw, gallery-owner Robert Ross, and artists James Muirhead Bone, William Rothenstein and Augustus John

1906 Visits New York briefly; marries Peggy Dunlop; settles at Stamford Bridge Studios, Fulham. Exhibits at the New English Art Club

1907 Moves studio to 72 Cheyne Walk, Chelsea. Begins work on the eighteen statues for Charles Holden's British Medical Association Building, the Strand; first *Romily John (ROM)*

1908 Controversy surrounds unveiling of BMA sculptures; commission for the *Tomb of Oscar Wilde* is announced

1909 First sculpture of Gypsy model, Nan Condron

1910 Becomes a naturalised British citizen on 22 December. Exhibits at the Allied Artists' Association at the Whitechapel Art Gallery. Attempts unsuccessfully, with Eric Gill, to establish an artists' commune with monumental sculpture at Asheham House, Sussex; first work purchased by public gallery; key works include *ROM*, *Sun Goddess, Crouching, Maternity* and *One of the Hundred Pillars of the Secret Temple*

1911 Exhibits at National Portrait Society, London; works include *Nan the Dreamer*

1912 Begins first series of portraits of Peggy; introduces Mark Gertler to Egyptian art at the British Museum; meets Wyndham Lewis. Completes *Tomb of Oscar Wilde* which Gaudier Brzeska views in studio. Whilst installing it in Paris meets Modigliani, Brancusi, Picasso and the collector Paul Guillaume; probably purchases first pieces of primitive sculpture. On returning to London exhibits *Maternity* at Allied Artists Association; friendship with Gill breaks up; moves to Pett Level, Sussex, whilst keeping rooms above Harold Munro's Poetry Bookshop

1913 In January travels with David Bomberg to Paris where he sees Brummer Fang Reliquary Head (purchased in 1935). In London begins *Rock Drill* and has first one-man show at Twenty One Gallery. Exhibits in *Post-Impressionist and Futurist Exhibition* and at *International Exhibition of Modern Art* (Armory Show) in New York. Defended by T E Hulme in *New Age*. Other key works include *Study for Man Woman* and *Doves*

1914 To Paris for unveiling of *Tomb of Oscar Wilde* to hostile reception. In London exhibits in Jewish Section of *Twentieth Century Art: A Review of Modern Movements* at the Whitechapel Art Gallery. *Studies of Birth* illustrated in first issue of BLAST (cat no 52). Works exhibited at home of Lord Drogheda

1915 *Doves* purchased by John Quinn, New York collector / lawyer (who defined 'art' for United States Tariff Law)

1916 Returns from Pett Level to 23 Guildford Street, Bloomsbury. Exhibits *Rock Drill*

1917 Sells £1,600 worth of bronzes at first Leicester Galleries exhibition. Begins *Risen Christ*, prior to enlisting in Jewish 38th Battalion of the Royal Fusiliers, stationed in Plymouth. Fails to obtain War Artist appointment

1918 Absent without leave on eve of departure of regiment; hospitalised and invalided out of army. Begins series of portraits of first child, Peggy Jean. Produces several sculptures of Meum Lindsell Stewart

1920 Contemplates modelling a Deposition group. Attracts controversy when *Risen Christ* is seen by huge crowds at the Leicester Galleries. First illustrated monograph by Bernard van Dieren is published

1921 Works discussed in Kineton Parkes *Sculpture of Today* and attacked in Lorado Taft's *Modern Tendencies in Sculpture*. Meets Kathleen Garman and Henry Moore. Sculpts bust of fellow Jewish artist Jacob Kramer

1922 Commissioned to carve *W H Hudson Memorial* in London; rents cottage in Loughton, Essex

1923 First design for Hudson memorial is replaced by one based on the character of Rima from *Green Mansions*. Criticises restoration of British Museum's Greek and Roman sculptures

1924 Rejected as candidate for Chair of Sculpture at Royal College of Art. Work attacked by Roger Fry in *New Statesman*; anti-semitic article in *New Age*; writes foreword to Hulme's *Speculations*, edited by Herbert Read. Son Theo is born. He meets Indian sisters Sunita and Anita who become his models

1925 *W H Hudson Memorial* is unveiled by Prime Minister to most virulent criticism of his career including anti-semitic comments in the press and questions in Parliament. *Jacob Epstein* by Hubert Wellington is published with 35 plates. Meets Matthew Smith who becomes a lifelong friend

1926 Exhibits *Visitation* at the Leicester Galleries

1927 Gives up Guildford Street studio; moves to New York for four months to attend successful exhibition at Ferargil Gallery. Meets William Zorach, visits Barnes Collection in Philadelphia and defends Brancusi at a Customs' hearing. Birth of daughter Kitty

1928 Returns to London, moving to 18 Hyde Park Gate. Invited to carve *Night and Day* on London Underground Electric Railways Headquarters; purchases *Baby Suckling* from Henry Moore's first one-man show. Own work discussed in *Some Modern Sculptors* by Stanley Casson

1929 Begins carving *Genesis*; studies of Sunita and other exotic models are published in *Epstein Seventy Five Drawings* by Hubert Wellington. Birth of daughter Esther. Key works include *Day and Night*

1930 Brings a court case against plagiarists; key works include *Genesis*

1931 Exhibits *Genesis* to a vituperative press; buys works by Henry Moore; resumes work on *Sun God* relief begun in 1910, and carves primeval Gods on the reverse. His work is discussed in Kineton Parkes *The Art of Carved Sculpture*, and in *The Sculptor Speaks*, a series of conversations with Arnold Haskell, who notes Epstein's ownership of over 200 pieces of primitive sculpture

1932 Exhibits Old Testament watercolours at the Redfern Gallery, London. Purchases Fang reliquary figure from De Mire sale and Moore's *Cosmopolitan*. His work is described in L. B. Powell *Jacob Epstein* and R H Wilenski *The Meaning of Modern Sculpture*

1933 Illustrates *The Book of Affinity* by Moysheh Oved (pseudonym of Edward Good). Paints nearly 100 watercolours of Epping Forest. Excluded as an 'alien' from Eric Underwood's *A Short History of English Sculpture*

1934 Begins carving *Ecce Homo (Behold the Man)*

1935 Son Jackie is born. Purchases the Fang Head from Joseph Brummer. Begins drop-curtain for ballet *David*; Southern Rhodesian Government announces its intention to remove the BMA statues; *Hudson Memorial* is defiled by the Independent Fascist League and *Behold the Man* is attacked by the Catholic press but defended by Anthony Blunt in *The Spectator*

1936 Carves *Consummatum Est* and begins illustrations for Baudelaire's *Fleurs du Mal*

1937 Signs with Gill, Moore, Herbert Read and Paul Nash a letter of co-operation with the International Peace Campaign against Fascist aggression in Spain; the BMA statues are mutilated despite public protest; *Consummatum Est* is attacked by the press and clergy; Moore's *Mother and Child* is described as 'Epstein the Morning after the Night Before'

1938 Receives an honorary degree from Aberdeen University; with Moore, Stephen Spender and others refused a visa to travel to Republican Spain; begins carving *Adam*; shows *Fleurs du Mal* drawings unsuccessfully at Tooth's, London

1939 *Adam* is exhibited at the Leicester Galleries; the public flocks to see it touring the country under new ownership. Financial difficulties force Epstein to sell his collection of Matthew Smith paintings

1940 Begins carving *Jacob and the Angel*; *Adam* exhibited in New York; *Flowers of Evil* and Epsteins's autobiography, *Let There Be Sculpture*, are published

1942 *Jacob and the Angel* at the Leicester Galleries; shares two-man show with Matthew Smith at Temple Newsam, Leeds; Leeds City Art Gallery purchases *Lady Gregory* and *Peggy Jean Laughing*. Robert Black *The Art of Jacob Epstein* is published

1944 Begins work on *Lucifer*; is omitted from A T Broadbent *Sculpture Today in Great Britain*

1945 Welcomed by Picasso at a party for Felix Topolski in London; *Lucifer* is exhibited at the Leicester Galleries then rejected as a gift by both the Tate Gallery and the Fitzwilliam Museum, Cambridge

1946 Models portrait of Winston Churchill

1947 Begins carving *Lazarus*; *Lucifer* presented to Birmingham City Gallery; Margaret Epstein dies

1948 *Girl with Gardenias* (Kathleen Garman) is shown at the first *Sculpture in the Open Air* exhibition at Battersea Park, London

1949 Visits New York briefly; *Youth Advancing* is commissioned for the Festival of Britain

1950 Commissioned to make *Madonna and Child* for the Convent of the Holy Child Jesus in Cavendish Square, London

1951 Portraits of T S Eliot and W Somerset Maugham; visits Philadelphia to discuss commission for Social Consciousness. *Youth Advancing* shown at the Festival of Britain; *Lazarus* is displayed in Battersea Park

1952 Retrospective organised by Arts Council is held at Tate Gallery; *Lazarus* is unveiled at New College Chapel, Oxford

1953 Opens the London County Council Sculpture School at Camberwell; receives an honorary doctorate from Oxford University; refuses membership of the Royal Society of British Sculptors. Commissioned to make *Christ in Majesty* for Llandaff Cathedral and *Field Marshal Smuts* for Parliament Square, London. Cavendish Square *Madonna and Child* is unveiled

1954 Receives knighthood; begins the *Liverpool Resurgent* for Lewis's Store and speaks on BBC Radio ('Sir Jacob Epstein on Modern Art'); his son Theo dies and his daughter Esther commits suicide

1955 Marries Kathleen Garman (Lady Epstein); they travel to Philadelphia for the unveiling of *Social Consciousness*; the *Trades Union Congress War Memorial*, London and *St Michael* and the *Devil* for Coventry Cathedral are commissioned; *Epstein: an Autobiography* is published; *Liverpool Resurgent* and *Field Marshal Smuts* unveiled

1956 *Memorial to William Blake* is commissioned for Poets' Corner, Westminster Abbey

1957 *Christ in Majesty* and *William Blake* unveiled; *Epstein: A Camera Study of the Sculptor at Work* by Geoffrey Ireland (introduction by Laurie Lee) is published

1958 Ill in hospital with pleurisy and a thrombosis; unable to attend unveiling of *TUC War Memorial*; convalesces in France and Northern Italy, visiting Padua where he sees Donatello's *Gatamelata*. *Ascension of Christ* commissioned for Crownhill Church, Plymouth; HRH Princess Margaret sits for her portrait; the parishioners of Selby Abbey, Yorkshire, petition to reject the gift of *Behold the Man*; *Bowater House Group* begun

1959 Models posthumous portrait of *David Lloyd George* for the Houses of Parliament; completes *Bowater House Group* on day of his death, 19 August, at Hyde Park Gate; buried at Putney Vale Cemetery; memorial service held at St Paul's Cathedral. 'We have lost a great sculptor' (Moore's obituary notice, *The Sunday Times*, 23 August)

Dora Gordine Abbreviated Chronology:

We are grateful to Dr Jonathan Black for the preparation of this chronology

26 April 1898 Born Dora Gordin in the Latvian port of Liepaja (also known as Libau). At the time Latvia was a province within the Russian Empire. Father was Mark Gordin, a Russian of Scottish ancestry, who worked as an architect and civil engineer. Dora had one elder brother, Leopold (1893-1979) and two elder sisters; one of them was called Anna

1912 The Gordin family was living in Revel (now known as Tallinn), Estonia. The city was an important naval base for the Imperial Russian Baltic Fleet

1914 Russia declared war on Germany

1917 Russian Revolution in Petrograd/St. Petersburg. Tsar Nicholas II was forced to abdicate. The Provisional Government of Alexander Kerensky was overthrown by the Bolsheviks

1918 Mark Gordin died from a stroke after being threatened by Red Guards in Revel

1919 Leopold Gordin worked in Revel as an Interpreter between the Transport Section of General Yudenitch's White 'North-Western Army' and the British Military Mission to Estonia. He was also employed by the American Relief Organisation's European Children's Fund in Revel and may have found Gordine a job with that body

1920 An independent Estonia signed a peace treaty with the Bolshevik government. White Russians were encouraged to leave Estonian territory. Leopold Gordin left Revel to resume his interrupted studies at Edinburgh University. Dora, her mother and sister Anna also left Revel, but travelled to Berlin

1920-24 Lived in Berlin, where she studied music and met the influential art dealer Alfred Flechtheim

1924 Moved to Paris to begin a career as a sculptor. She may have studied part-time at the École des Beaux-Arts and at the Académie de la Grande Chaumière. She experimented first with woodcarvings, and then concentrated on modelling in clay for bronzes to be cast using the so-called 'lost-wax' method

1925 Employed as a part-time painter in the British Pavilion at the Exposition Internationale des Arts Décoratifs et Industriels Modernes in Paris. Exhibited, for the first time as 'Dora Gordine', a *Bronze* at the Nation Salon in Paris. She gave her nationality as 'Estonian' and her address as 'Maison des Étudiants, 214 Boulevard Raspail'. Had met the celebrated sculptor Aristide Maillol (1861-1944) who was impressed by her work and advised her not to continue her sculptural training at an art school: 'Work where you can, and how you can, but work alone'

1926 Introduced to Janet Vaughan (1899-1993) by David Gourlay – co-owner of the Wayfarers' Travel Agency, which had an office in

Paris. Gordine often stayed with Vaughan, then a medical student, in her room at 19 Taviton Street, Bloomsbury. Later that year Vaughan introduced Gordine to the Honourable Richard Hare (1907-1966), second son of the Earl of Listowel and then a student at Balliol College, Oxford. Hare quickly asked Gordine to marry him but she refused because she first wanted to establish herself as a successful sculptor

1926 Encouraged by the established sculptors François Pompon (1855-1933) and Antoine Bourdelle (1861-1929) Gordine exhibited two bronzes at the Salon des Tuileries, Paris: *Head of a Chinaman* (later known as *The Chinese Philosopher*) and *Torso*. Both works were cast by the prestigious Valsuani Foundry at 74 rue des Plantes. She continued to use Valsuani for the next thirteen years

1927 *Head of a Chinaman* was exhibited with the Royal Scottish Academy in Edinburgh. This was the first occasion Gordine exhibited within Great Britain. First major article on Gordine was published in the prominent French arts magazine *L'Amour de l'Art* by the leading art critic Marie Dormoy

1928 First appreciation of Gordine's work in English was published in the arts magazine *Drawing and Design* by its editor Gerald Reitlinger. Exhibited 17 bronzes, alongside the painter C.R.W. Nevinson, at the Leicester Galleries, Irving Street, London. The 'note' to her catalogue was written by George Eumorfopoulos, an important collector of Oriental Art. A cast of one of her exhibits, *Male Torso*, was bought by the Colonial Office for Achimota College, Accra, Ghana (then known as 'The Gold Coast')

1929 The French architect Auguste Perret (1874-1954) built a studio-home for Gordine at 21 rue du Belvédère in the Château Les Princes-Marmottan quartier of the Parisian municipality of Boulogne-Billancourt. Exhibited sixteen bronzes with two German painters, Fritz Kronenberg and Paul Strecker, at the Galérie Alfred Flechtheim, Berlin
Breton Head and *Mongolian Head* were included in the exhibition 'Modern and African Sculpture' at the Sydney Burney Gallery, London. Other exhibitors included: Zadkine; Maillol; Epstein; Hepworth; Skeaping and Dobson, alongside carvings from: Dahomy; Gabon; Nigeria; Benin and the Congo

1930 Arrived in Singapore having sailed from Italy via the Suez Canal. She then moved to live in the town of Johore Bahru, capital of the Unfederated Malay State of Johore.
The Singapore Municipal Commissioners invited Gordine to provide six bronzes for the interior of the recently completed Municipal Buildings (now the Parliament Building)
Married Dr. George Herbert Garlick (1886-1958), then Deputy Chief Medical Officer of the Johore Medical Service, at a Registry Office in Singapore

1931 Travelled through Malaya, Cambodia and Thailand

1932 Visited the Dutch East Indies (now Indonesia), including Bali, Shanghai and Peking
Gordine and her husband sailed from Singapore for France. The *Straits Times* published a lengthy article on Gordine's sculpture by Sir Richard Winstedt – then General Adviser to the Sultan of Johore

1933 Gordine exhibited 15 bronzes at the Leicester Galleries, London, alongside the American painter Edward Bruce. Dr Garlick did not attend the private view having already returned to Singapore. Returned to Johore via Paris. 3 Gordines, 2 Epsteins and 2 Maillols included in *Summer Exhibition of Drawings, Paintings and Sculptures* at the Leicester Galleries, London

1934 Richard Hare wrote to the architect Godfrey Samuel (1904-1982), whom he had befriended at Oxford, asking him to design a house for Gordine on Merton Lane, Highgate

1935 Gordine arrived in London, from Singapore, without her husband. Richard Hare, on Gordine's behalf, purchased a plot of land on Kingston Hill on which a house she had largely designed would be built. The house will be called 'Dorich House' – a composite of Dora and Richard

1936 Gordine rented a flat at 60 Church Street (now Old Church Street), Chelsea. Gordine and Richard Hare were married at the Chelsea Registry Office. Shortly thereafter they moved into Dorich House. On the marriage licence Gordine stated she was a spinster and gave her birth year as 1906

1937 Exhibited *Cingalese Girl* and *Male Torso* [*Dyak*] at the Royal Academy, London. She exhibited regularly at the Academy for the next 23 years. The President of the Royal Institute of British Architects [RIBA], H.S. Goodhart Rendel, commissioned a bronze portrait head from Gordine of H S E Vanderpant, Lord Mayor of Westminster and a benefactor of the Institute

1938 Gordine was elected an Associate Member of the Royal Society of British Sculpture [RBS] along with Frank Dobson, Eric Gill, Thomas Huxley-Jones and Maurice Lambert. H S E Vanderpant presented Gordine's bronze *Seated Baby*, which he commissioned, to the Westminster City Council Maternity and Child Welfare Centre and Day Nursery on Bessborough Street, London, SW1
Exhibition at the Leicester Galleries comprising 30 bronzes and 21 drawings. The catalogue essay was written by the painter, art historian and critic D.S. MacColl (1859-1948) who earlier in 1938 sat to Gordine for a portrait head. The exhibition was both a critical and a financial success

1939 Gordine's *Torso* (now known as *Walking Male Torso*) was presented to the University of London by a group of Gordine's supporters including H S Goodhart Rendel (President of the RIBA) and Sir William Reid Dick (recently President of the RBS and Sculptor to King George VI). The statue was placed on display inside the lift hall of Senate House on Malet Street, London

1940 Represented in an exhibition of British Art for war charities held at the Stafford Gallery, 13 St. James's Place, London. Other exhibitors included: Jacob Epstein, Barbara Hepworth, John Skeaping, Gertrude Hermes, Maurice Lambert, Elsa Fraenkel and Dora Clarke.
Lectured to the Royal Asiatic Society on 'The Beauty of Asiatic Sculpture'

1942 Unsuccessful attempts to be appointed an official war artist by the War Artists Advisory Committee [WAAC] of the Ministry of Information and be elected an Associate of the Royal Academy.
Lectured to the Royal Asiatic Society on 'The Indonesian Sculpture of Indo-China and Java' at the Royal Empire Society Building

1943 Lectured on 'Indian Sculpture' at the School of Oriental

Studies (later the School of Oriental and African Studies), University of London. Broke her wrist in a fall while working on a head of Sir Kenneth Clark, then Director of the National Gallery

1944 Began to use the Morris Singer Foundry of Lambeth to cast her work. She would use the Foundry for the next thirty years. Lecture on 'The Indian Influence on the Sculpture of Java, Siam and Indo-China' for the Royal India Society

1945 Exhibited 28 pieces of sculpture (25 bronzes, 2 plasters and 1 in silver pewter) at the Leicester Galleries with William Roberts and Henry Lamb. One Gordine work included in group show at Leicester Galleries with, among others, four Epsteins and one Maillol

1946 Bronze relief portrait of *Sun Yat Sen* (1866-1925), first President of the Chinese Republic, was unveiled in Warwick Court, Gray's Inn Place, London. Gordine's *Girl with Pigtail* included alongside Epstein's *Rani Rama* in *Artists of Fame and Promise* at Leicester Galleries, London

1947 Visited the United States with her husband – who had been awarded a one year Fellowship by the Rockefeller Foundation, to develop 'Slavic Studies' at the Hoover Institute, Stanford University, California. She lived for a while in Los Angeles, developed contacts with Hollywood and gave several lectures on sculpture to women's groups

1948 Discussed her sculpture on the BBC Television programme 'Designed for Women'

1949 Contributed work to the Arts Council exhibition 'Open Air Sculpture' in Battersea Park. Elected a Fellow of the RBS. Exhibited 32 pieces of sculpture (31 bronzes and 1 plaster) at the Leicester Galleries, London. This will be her last solo exhibition

1950 Nominated to become an ARA but did not win sufficient votes. Contributed to *The Observer Exhibition: Portraits of Children* at the Royal Watercolour Society Galleries. Other exhibitors included: Jacob Epstein, Daphne Hardy, Karin Jonzen, Willi Soukop, Frank Dobson and Anthony Caro

1951 *Male Torso* [*Dyak*] was displayed at the Festival of Britain, under an arch of Hungerford Bridge, facing the entrance of the British Transport Pavilion. Sold her studio-house, at 21 rue du Belvédère. She gave her birthdate as 26 April 1898 and birthplace as 'Libau, Lettonie'

1952 Contributed to an exhibition of contemporary sculpture organised by the International Faculty of Arts and held at 45 Park Lane. Other exhibitors included: Jacob Epstein; Karen Jonzen; F E McWilliam; Wili Soukop; Reg Butler and Henry Moore

1953 First Exhibition of the Society of Portrait Sculptors [SPS], Imperial Institute Art Gallery, London. Gordine was a founder member of the Society along with: Gilbert Ledward; Charles Wheeler; Arthur Fleischmann; Jacob Epstein and Frank Dobson. She exhibited annually with the SPS up to 1959

1954 Bronze relief portrait of General Draza Mihailovic (1893-1946), leader of the Serbian Royalist chetniks was unveiled by Lady Leila Paget in St. Sava's Serbian Orthodox Church, Lancaster Road, Notting Hill, London

1956 A last and unsuccessful attempt to be elected an ARA

1957 Elected a Fellow of the Royal Society for the Encouragement of Arts. A bronze head of Lucien Pissarro (1863-1944), commissioned by his daughter Orovida, was unveiled at the Ashmolean Museum, Oxford

1958 Exhibited at the '26th Annual Exhibition of Artists of Fame and Promise', Leicester Galleries, London

1959 Visited Bloomington, Indiana with Richard Hare who had been appointed a temporary Visiting Professor in the Department of Slavic Languages and Literature at Indiana University

1960 Exhibited for the last time at the Royal Academy. Exhibited *Goddess of Health* (also known as *Iran*) at the Arts Council's 'Open Air Exhibition of Sculpture' at Battersea Park. Bronze low-relief *Power* was unveiled, by the Duke of Edinburgh, in the Administrative Block of the new Esso Petroleum Refinery at Milford Haven

1963 Bronze group *Mother and Child* was unveiled by Queen Elizabeth II in the entrance foyer of the Royal Marsden Hospital, Sutton, Surrey

1964 A second cast of *Mother and Child* was unveiled outside the Indianapolis Museum of Art

1966 Richard Hare, now Professor of Russian Literature at the School of Slavonic and Eastern European Studies, University of London, died at Dorich House from a heart attack

1972 An interview with Nancy Wise was broadcast on BBC Radio 4

1977 Ceased casting work with Morris Singer

1981 *Guadeloupe Head* was included in 'British Sculpture in the Twentieth Century', Whitechapel Art Gallery

1986 *Chinese Philosopher; Kwa Nin (Chinese Lady of Peace)* and *Malay Sultana* were exhibited in 'Sculpture in Britain Between the Wars', Fine Art Society, London

1987 Gordine opened Dorich House to the public

1988 In a burglary objets d'art worth £100,000 were stolen from Dorich House

1990 Interviewed by David Fraser Jenkins and Derek Pullen of the Tate Gallery

29 December 1991 Gordine died from a massive stroke at Dorich House

1997 *Dorothy Tutin* (in the role of Ibsen's Hedwig) exhibited with the Society of Portrait Sculptors, 28 Cork Street, London

2004 *Guadeloupe Head; Mongolian Head; Malay Sultana* and *Javanese Head* exhibited in 'Head to Head', Tate Modern, London. Dorich House accorded Museum Status by Resource: The Council for Museums, Archives and Libraries

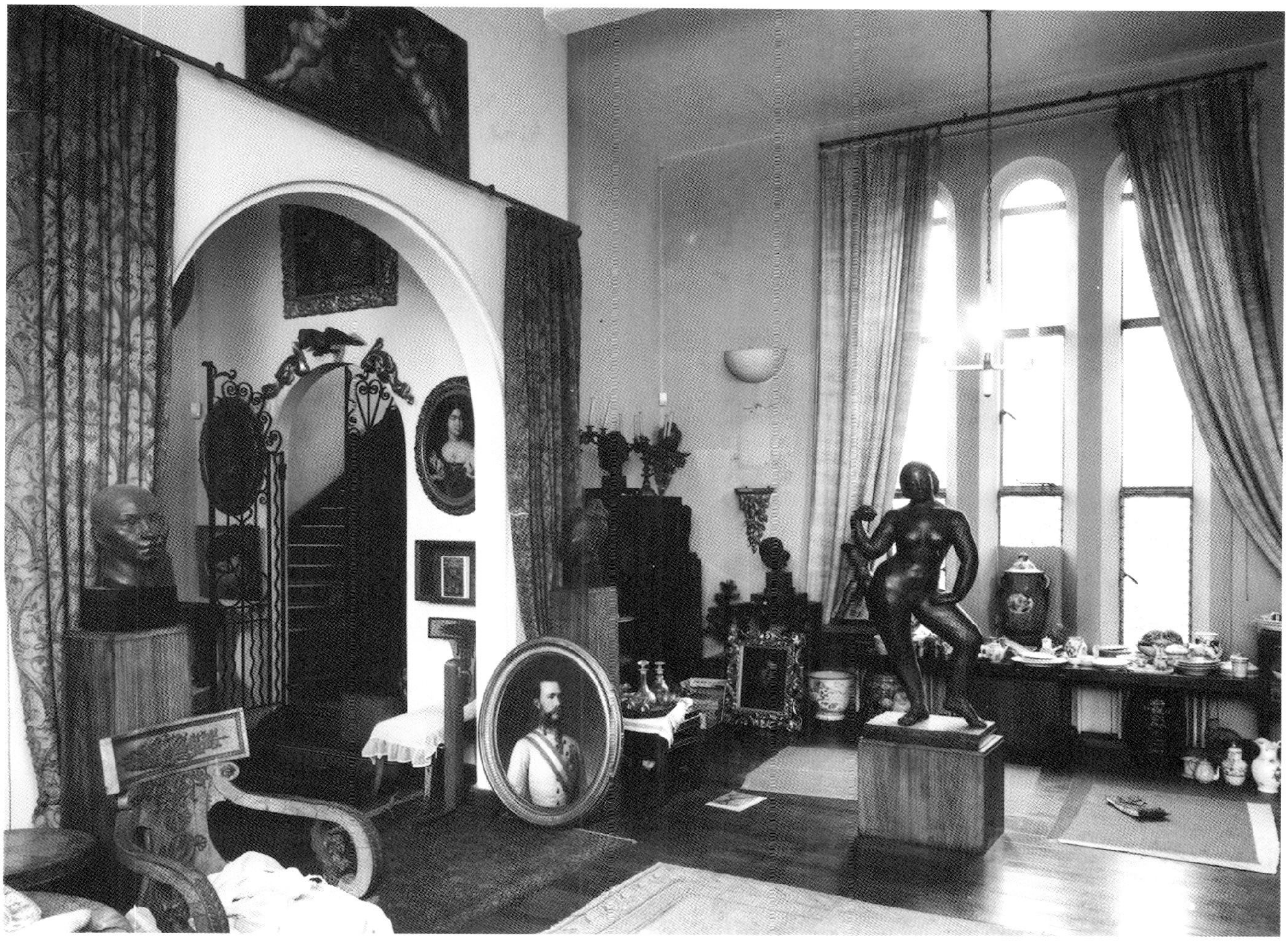

Fig. 31 *The Living Room at Dorich House,* 1949

Concise bibliography

Jacob Epstein: A Select Bibliography

Compiled by Sarah MacDougall

Collection Catalogues

Anon., *The Garman-Ryan Collection: Illustrated Catalogue* (Walsall: Walsall Metropolitan Borough Library and Museum Services, 1976)

Bassani, E and McLeod, M D *Jacob Epstein: Collector* (Milan: Associazione Poro, 1989)

Epstein, J *The Jacob Epstein collection in the Baltimore Museum of Art* (Baltimore: Baltimore Museum of Art, 1939)

Silber, E *The Sculpture of Epstein with a Complete Catalogue* (Oxford: Phaidon Press, 1986)

Exhibition Catalogues

2002 Anon., *Focus on the Collection: Jacob Epstein* (Jerusalem: Israel Museum, 2002)

2002 Katz, A *Jacob Epstein 1880-1959: Bronze Sculptures, Les Fleurs du Mal Drawings and Other Works on Paper* (London: Boundary Gallery, 2002)

1998 Inverness Museum and Art Gallery *The Rock Drill and Beyond: An Exhibition featuring Rock Drill, 1913, by Jacob Epstein* (Inverness: Inverness Museum and Art Gallery, 1998)

1998 Various authors *Carving Mountains: Modern Stone Sculpture in England 1907-37: Frank Dobson, Jacob Epstein, Henri Gaudier-Brzeska, Eric Gill, Barbara Hepworth, Henry Moore, Ben Nicholson, John Skeaping* (Cambridge: Kettle's Yard, 1998)

1992 *The Flower Paintings: Sir Jacob Epstein* (London: David Messum, 1992)

1989 Chapman, K and Barker, E *Jacob Epstein (1880-1959): A Vision of Women* (London: Chapman Gallery, 1989)

1989 *Father and Son [Epstein, Sir Jacob & Garman, Theodore]* (London: Fine Art Society, 1989)

1987 *Jacob Epstein, 1880-1959 : Drawings, Paintings, Sculpture* (London: Montpelier Studio, 1987)

1987 Silber, E *Jacob Epstein: Sculpture and Drawings* (Leeds: Maney in association with the Henry Moore Centre for the Study of Sculpture,1987, republished 1989)

1987 Katz, A *Jacob Epstein: Drawings and Illustrations* (London: Boundary Gallery, 1987)

1981 Buckle, R, ed., *Epstein: Edinburgh Festival Society Memorial Exhibition*, (Edinburgh: Edinburgh Festival Society, 1981)

1980 *Sir Jacob Epstein Centenary: Tate Gallery, November & December 1980* (London: Tate Gallery, 1980)

1980 *Epstein Centenary 1980: Bronzes, Drawings and Watercolours* (London: Ben Uri Art Gallery, 1980)

1980 d'Offay, A *Jacob Epstein, 1880-1959* (London: Anthony d'Offay, 1980)

1980 Silber, E *Rebel Angel: Sculpture and Watercolours by Sir Jacob Epstein 1880-1959* (Birmingham: Birmingham Museums & Art Gallery, 1980)

1973 *Sculpture of Jacob Epstein: the Eisenberg-Robbins Collection* (Washington, DC: Corcoran Gallery of Art, 1973)

1973 *Jacob Epstein: The Rock Drill period (London: Anthony d'Offay*, 1973)

1971 *An Exhibition of Sculpture and Drawings from 1900-1932 by Sir Jacob Epstein* (London: Ernest Brown & Phillips,1971)

1970 Schinman, E P, and Schinman, B A, eds., *Jacob Epstein: A Catalogue of the Collection of Edward P. Schinman* (Rutherford, N J: Fairleigh Dickinson University Press, 1970)

1968 *Jacob Epstein: Retrospective Exhibition of Sculpture and Drawings* (London: London Arts Group, 1968)

1967 *British Painting 1900-1950: including eight paintings by Stanley Spencer and Work by William Brooker, Jacob Epstein, Sylvia Gosse* (London: Arthur Tooth & Sons, 1967)

1966 Mercury Gallery *Jacob Epstein: Drawings, Watercolours, Sculpture* (London: Mercury Gallery, 1966)

1965 Rye Art Gallery *Jacob Epstein: Sculpture, Paintings and Drawings* (Rye: Rye Art Gallery, 1965)

1965 Tib Lane Gallery *Jacob Epstein, 1880-1959; Henri Gaudier-Brzeska, 1891-1915* (Manchester: Tib Lane Gallery, 1965)

1964 Arthur Tooth & Sons *Augustus John, Paul Nash, Walter Sickert, Matthew Smith, Stanley Spencer, Jacob Epstein: Paintings, Drawings, Watercolours, Sculpture* (London: Arthur Tooth & Sons, 1964)

1962 Fulford, R T B et al *4 Exhibitions to celebrate the Opening of Abbot Hall Art Gallery. Daniel Gardner, 1750-1805. Seven Modern British Painters. Bronzes by Sir Jacob Epstein. First Acquisitions. 28th September to 9th November.* (Kendal: Abbot Hall Art Gallery, 1962)

1961 Brown Thomas & Co., Little Theatre *Loaned Exhibition of Bronzes and Water colours by Epstein: in the Little Theatre, Brown Thomas & Co.*, September 26th, 1961 (Dublin: Little Theatre, Brown Thomas, 1961)

1961 *Jacob Epstein: Retrospective Exhibition of Sculpture and Drawings* (London: R. Stockwell, 1961)

Epstein (London: Arts Council, 1961)

1961 Auckland City Art Gallery *Jacob Epstein: Drawings and Sculpture; Auckland City Art Gallery, March-April 1961* (Auckland, NZ: Pelorus Press, 1961)

1960 Epstein, Sir J, and Haskell, A L. *Fifty years of Bronzes and Drawings by Sir Jacob Epstein (1880-1959)* (London: Ernest Brown & Phillips, 1960)

1960 Epstein, J and Fagg, W (introduction) *The Epstein Collection of Tribal and Exotic Sculpture* (London: Arts Council, 1960)

1959 Ben Uri Art Gallery *Sir Jacob Epstein, 1880-1959: Exhibition of Bronzes, November 25th-December 22nd, 1959* (London: Ben Uri Art Gallery, 1959)

1959 Epstein, J, Thompson, Sir A F *Bronzes & Drawings by Epstein: from the Arnold F Thompson Collection* (Nottingham: Victoria Street Art Gallery, 1959)

1959 *Sculpture: Ten Modern Masters ... [etc.]* (Toronto: The Galleries, 1959)

1959 Sutherland, G; Epstein, Sir J; Hutton, J *An exhibition in the Chapel of Unity of Tapestry by Graham Sutherland, Sculpture by Sir Jacob Epstein, Glass by John Hutton for the New Cathedral* (Coventry: Coventry Cathedral, 1959)

1953 *Catalogue of an Exhibition of Recent Portraits by Jacob Epstein* (London: Ernest Brown & Phillips, 1953)

1952 Arts Council of Great Britain/Tate Gallery *Epstein: An Exhibition held at the Tate Gallery* (London: Arts Council of Great Britain, 1952)

1950 *Landscapes in Oil and Water-colour by Ethelbert White: A New Carving, "Lazarus" and Other Recent Sculpture by Jacob Epstein* (London: Ernest Brown & Phillips, 1950)

1947 *Exhibition of English & Continental Paintings with Sculptures by Jacob Epstein* (London: Stoke Newington Public Libraries, 1947)

1947 *Landscapes in Oil and Water-colour by Ethelbert White: New Sculpture by Jacob Epstein* (London: Ernest Brown & Phillips, 1947)

1945 *Jacob Epstein:, "Lucifer" and other paintings of flowers and landscapes of Epping Forest [Drawings illustrating "Quest for Sita" by Maurice Collis]* (London: Ernest Brown & Phillips, 1945)

1944 *Pastels by a Group of Artists; Flowers and landscapes of Epping Forest by Jacob Epstein* (London: Ernest Brown & Phillips, 1944)

1944 *"Girl with the Gardenias" and Other Recent Sculpture by Jacob Epstein; Paintings and drawings by John Craxton; Paintings by J.B. Manson* (London: Ernest Brown & Phillips, 1944)

1943 Lakeland Garage *Catalogue of Collection of Sculpture in Bronze by Epstein and Exhibition of Paintings by Contemporary British Artists* (Windermere: Merchant Navy Comforts Service Committee, 1943)

1942 *"Jacob and the Angel" and New Bronzes by Jacob Epstein; Recent paintings by Dod Procter* (London: Ernest Brown & Phillips, 1942)

1942 *Jacob Epstein: Exhibition of Paintings of Dahlias, Sunflowers and Landscapes* (London: Ernest Brown & Phillips, 1942)

1942 *Exhibition of Sculpture and Paintings by Jacob Epstein and Matthew Smith* (Leeds: Leeds City Art Gallery & Temple Newsam, 1942)

1940 *Flower Paintings and Some New Bronzes by Jacob Epstein* (London: Ernest Brown & Phillips, 1940)

1939 *New Sculpture and Drawings of Children by Jacob Epstein* (London: Ernest Brown & Phillips, 1939)

1939 Smith, M *Catalogue of a Retrospective Exhibition of Paintings by Matthew Smith: the Collection of Jacob Epstein* (London: Ernest Brown & Phillips 1939)

1938 *An Exhibition of Drawings by Jacob Epstein for 'Les Fleurs du Mal' of Charles Baudelaire* (London: Arthur Tooth & Sons, 1938)

1937 *Sculpture by Jacob Epstein* (London: Ernest Brown & Phillips, 1937)

1936 *Flower paintings: An Exhibition of New Watercolours by Jacob Epstein* (London: Arthur Tooth & Sons, 1936)

1935 *An Exhibition of Carving and Bronzes by Jacob Epstein* (London: Ernest Brown & Phillips, 1935)

1933 *Watercolours of Epping Forest by Jacob Epstein* (London: Arthur Tooth & Sons, 1933)

1933 *Carvings and Bronzes by Jacob Epstein* (London: Ernest Brown & Phillips, 1933)

1932 *Illustrations to the Old Testament by Epstein* (London: Redfern Gallery, 1932)

1931 *An Exhibition of New Sculpture by Jacob Epstein* (London: Ernest Brown & Phillips, 1931)

1930 *Drawings and Sculpture by Some Contemporary Sculptors: Jacob Epstein, Frank Dobson, Henry Moore, Henri Gaudier-Brzeska (1891-1915)* (London: Zwemmer Gallery, 1930)

1928 *Drawings by Epstein* (London: Godfrey Phillips, 1928)

1926 *An Exhibition of New Work in Sculpture by Jacob Epstein* (London: Ernest Brown & Phillips, 1926)

1924 *An Exhibition of New Sculpture by Jacob Epstein* (London: Ernest Brown & Phillips, 1924)

1920 *An Exhibition of Recent Sculpture by Jacob Epstein* (London: Ernest Brown & Phillips, 1920)

1917 *An Exhibition of Water-colours and Drawings by a Group of Artists Serving with His Majesty's Forces: including Recent Sculpture by Jacob Epstein* (London: Ernest Brown & Phillips, 1917)

Biographical

Babson, J F *The Epsteins: A Family Album* (Bucks: Aylesbury: Taylor Hall Publishing, 1986)

Buckle, R *Jacob Epstein: Sculptor* (London: Faber and Faber, 1963)

Connolly, C *The Rare and the Beautiful: The Lives of the Garmans* (London: Harper Collins, 2004)

Epstein, Sir J *Let There Be Sculpture: The Autobiography of Jacob Epstein* (London: Michael Joseph, 1940)

Gardiner, S *Epstein: Artist Against the Establishment* (London: Michael Joseph, 1992)

Rose, J *Daemons and Angels: A Life of Jacob Epstein* (London: Constable, 2002)

Other

Barker, E *New Light on Epstein's Early Career* [Figures (destroyed) on the facade of the B.M.A. building, 1907-8] (London: *Burlington Magazine*, Vol. 130, 1988)

Baudelaire, C P; Epstein J; Laver J *Flowers of Evil, Translated into English Verse by Various Hands*. Edited, with an introduction and notes, by James Laver, and illustrated with drawings by Jacob Epstein (London: Printed for members of the Limited Editions Club at the Fanfare Press, 1940)

Black, R *Art of Jacob Epstein* (Cleveland, OH: World Publishing Co., 1942)

Cork, R *Jacob Epstein* (London: Tate Gallery Publishing, 1999)

Dolitski Menahem Mendel; Hapgood Hutchins; Epstein Jacob; Rosenfeld Morris; Wald Abraham Zunser Eliakim *Four Poets of the Ghetto with 5 Charcoal Sketches by Jacob Epstein* (Berkeley Heights, NJ: Oriole Press, 1963)

Epstein, Sir J and Haskell, A L *The Sculptor Speaks: A Series of Conversations on Art* (London: William Heinemann, 1931)

Epstein Drawings: with notes by Lady Epstein, and an Introduction by Richard Buckle (London: Faber & Faber, 1962)

Epstein J *Seventy-five Drawings, etc.* (London: J. Saville & Co., 1929)

Epstein, J and Hapgood, H *The Spirit of the Ghetto: Studies of the Jewish Quarter of New York,* Revised edition, (New York; London: Funk and Wagnalls, 1909)

Friedman, T/Henry Moore Centre for the Study of Sculpture *'The Hyde Park atrocity': Epstein's Rima: Creation and Controversy* (Leeds, Yorkshire, England: Henry Moore Centre for the Study of Sculpture, Leeds City Art Galleries, 1988)

Goold, M *A Little Revolution: Direct Carving Revived: the Stonecarving Methods of Eric Gill and Jacob Epstein, 1907-1925* (Birmingham: University of Birmingham, 1989)

Groser, M; Farrer, A M *Epstein's Lazarus* (Oxford: New College, 1983)

Hulme, T E; Read, H; Epstein, Sir J, *Speculations: Essays on Humanism and the Philosophy of Art* (London: Routledge and Kegan Paul, 1924)

Ireland, G & Lee, L *Epstein 1956: A Camera Study of the Sculptor* (London: Lion & Unicorn Press, 1960)

Oyved, M *The Book of Affinity: Coloured Drawings by Jacob Epstein* (London: William Heinemann, 1933)

Peck, B "Another Thirty Years War: How the BMA – or Rhodesia – missed a half-million pound boat" in: *History of Medicine* Vol. 7, no. 1/2 (Spring/Summer 1976)

Pennington, M W *Jacob Epstein: The Years of Abstraction, 1909-1920* (M Litt thesis) (Edinburgh: University of Edinburgh, 1989)

Pennington, M *An Angel for a Martyr: Jacob Epstein's Tomb for Oscar Wilde* (Reading: Whiteknights Press, 1987)

Powell L B *Jacob Epstein* (London: Chapman & Hall, 1932)

Van Dieren, B *Epstein: Illustrated with fifty reproductions in collotype of the sculptor's work* (London & New York: John Lane, 1920)

Wellington, H and Rutherston, A D *Jacob Epstein* (London: Ernest Benn, 1925)

Dora Gordine: A Select Bibliography

Compiled by Dr Jonathan Black

Collection Catalogues

Martin, B *Dorich House Guidebook* (London: Kingston University Press, 2004) (Second Edition)

Martin, B *Dora Gordine Sculpture Collection* (London: Dorich House Museum, Kingston University, 2005)

Penny, N *Catalogue of European Sculpture in the Ashmolean Museum: 1540 to the Present Day. Volume III – British* (Oxford: Clarendon Press, 1992), p.93

Exhibition Catalogues

Anon., *Sculpture in the Open Air: Battersea Park June-September 1960* (London: The Arts Council, 1960), no.22

Brown, O 'Biographical Note', *Sculpture By Dora Gordine*, (London: Leicester Galleries, July 1933), p.8

Brown, O 'Biographical Note', *Sculpture By Dora Gordine* (London: Leicester Galleries, 1945), p.9

Brown, O 'Biographical Note', *Recent Sculpture including Figures from the Ballet by Dora Gordine* (London: Leicester Galleries, 1949), pp.3-4

Eumorfopoulos, G 'Introduction', *Catalogue Of An Exhibition Of Sculpture By Dora Gordine*, (London: Leicester Galleries, October 1928), p.3.

MacColl, D S 'Introduction', *Recent Sculpture And Drawings by Dora Gordine*, (London: Leicester Galleries, 1938), pp.5-8

Nairne, S and Serota, N *British Sculpture in the Twentieth Century* (London: Whitechapel Art Gallery, 1981)

Skipwith, P and Read, B *British Sculpture between the Wars* (London: Fine Art Society PLC, 1986), pp.84-5.

Newspapers, Magazines and Journals

Anon., 'Sculpture In Attap Studio. Miss Dora Gordine. Work Praised by Famous Critics', *The Straits Times*, 12 August 1930, p.14

Anon., '*The Bystander* Visits Dora Gordine At Dorich House, Kingston Vale', *The Bystander*, 28 February 1940, pp.266-7

Anon., 'This Is the House a Sculptor Built', *Ideal Home*, October 1946, pp.36-40

Anon., 'Life Worth Living', *Scope: The National Newspaper of Business and Industry*, April 1955, pp.80-3

Anon., 'Sculpture of Dora Gordine', *The Connoisseur*, February 1961, p.44

Anon., 'Dora Gordine's Great Bronze', *The Connoisseur*, June 1963, p.131

Anon., 'Dora Gordine' (Obituary), *The Daily Telegraph*, 2 January 1992, p.17

Anon., 'Dora Gordine' (Obituary), *The Times*, 3 January 1992, p.12

Barchan, P 'Dora Gordina', *Deutsche Kunst*, October 1929, pp.46-50

Barron, M 'Dorich House, Kingston Vale. Containing Miss Dora Gordine's Studio', *Country Life*, 5 November 1938, pp.456-7

Benoist, L 'Dora Gordine', *L'Amour de l'Art*, May 1929, pp.171-6

Collis, M 'The Leicester Galleries', *The Observer*, 21 October 1945, p.2

Cordier, L 'Pointes Sèches: Dora Gordine' *La Rumeur*, 22 July 1928, p.5

Dorment, R 'The Lost Generation: Sculpture in Britain between the Wars', *Country Life*, 3 July 1986, p.41

Dormoy, M 'Dora Gordine, Sculpteur', *L'Amour de l'Art*, No.5, May 1927, p.166

Gordine, D 'Angkor. Impressions of a Sculptor', *Bangkok Times*, 21 February 1931

Gordine, D 'The Beauty of Indian Sculpture', *The Journal of the Royal Asiatic Society*, January 1941, pp.42-8

Gordine, D 'The Sculpture of Indochina, Siam and Java', *The Journal of the Royal Asiatic Society*, April 1942, pp.132-138

Gordine, D 'Masterpieces of Oriental Art V: Chinese Sculpture', *The Journal of the Royal Asiatic Society*, October 1945, p.113

Gordine, D 'Masterpieces of Oriental Art VI: Ancient Egyptian Sculpture', *The Journal of the Royal Asiatic Society*, April 1946, p.3

Gordine, D 'Masterpieces of Oriental Art VII: Indian Sculpture', *The Journal of the Royal Asiatic Society*, December 1946, p.123.

Gordine, D 'Masterpieces of Oriental Art IX: Some Indian Sculpture at the Royal Academy', *The Journal of the Royal Asiatic Society*, December 1947, pp.139-141

Gordon, J 'Dora Gordine's Sculpture', *The Observer*, 6 November 1938, p.14.

Konody, P G 'Racial Types in Bronze. Amazing Studies by Girl Sculptor', *Daily Express*, 6 October 1928, p.3

Morrison, M 'Sculpture at the Royal Academy', *The Builder*, 30 May 1958, p.986

Newton, E 'The Galleries', *The Sunday Times*, 6 November 1938, p.5

Newton, E 'Craftsmanship', 30 October 1949, p.2

Nicholls, G A 'Beauty in Bronze', *Figure Quarterly* (American Edition), April 1956, pp.4-11

Reitlinger, G 'Paris Notes: Dora Gordine', *Drawing and Design*, Vol. IV, No. 20, February 1928, pp.33-5 and p.59

Rutter, F 'Dora Gordine', *The Sunday Times*, 9 July 1933, p.7

Sadler, Sir M, 'Art & Artists: The Leicester Galleries', *The Observer*, 9 July 1933, p.14

Skipwith, P 'Dora Gordine' (Obituary) *The Independent*, 4 January 1992, p.10

Sorrell, M 'Dora Gordine', *Apollo*, May 1949, pp.113-5

Symons, A 'Sculpture: Dora Gordine At The Leicester Galleries', *The Spectator*, 14 July 1933, pp.45-6

Symons, A 'The Work Of Dora Gordine', *The Spectator*, 4 November 1938, p.768

Tatlock, R R 'A Russian's Experiments: Dora Gordine', *Daily Telegraph*, 6 October 1928, p.15

Wallis, N 'At the Galleries', *The Observer*, 6 November 1949, p.6

Wilenski, R H 'Girl Sculptor Genius', *Evening Standard*, 5 October 1928, p.5

Winstedt, R O 'The Language of Plastic Beauty: An Appreciation of the Work of Dora Gordine', *The Straits Times*, 5 August 1932, p.10

Biographical

Nevinson, C R W *Paint and Prejudice*: The Life of An Artist (London: Methuen, 1937), pp.186-7

Stark, F *The Coast of Incense: Autobiography 1933-1939* (London: John Murray, 1953), p.238

Other:
Broadbent, A T *Sculpture Today in Great Britain: 1940-1943* (London: John Tiranti Ltd, 1944), p.13.

Martin, B 'Dora Gordine', in *Dictionary of Women Artists: Volume I Artists A-I*, edited by Delia Gaze (London and Chicago: Fitzroy Dearborn, 1997), pp.599-601

Martin, B 'A House of Her Own; Dora Gordine and Dorich House (1936)' in *Women's Places: Architecture and Design 1860-1960*, edited by Brenda Martin and Penny Sparke (London: Routledge, 2003), pp.125-147

Ramsden, E H *Twentieth Century Sculpture* (London: Pleiades, 1949), p.19

Short History of the Ben Uri Gallery

The Ben Uri was conceived in 1914 and founded in 1915 in the East End of London by the Russian-born Jewish artist Lazar Berson. A charismatic figure, he brought together a group of like-minded people from many different avenues of life who shared his aspiration "to form a permanent collection of works by Jewish artists that would enrich and ennoble the Jewish population" and "to offer a platform for Jewish artists, home and émigré, to exhibit and to demonstrate to the establishment and the wider public their potential contribution and influence" – a potential that was, and continues to be, richly fulfilled.

As a result of Berson's vision, the Ben Uri houses the world's largest and most important collection of its kind and continues to actively acquire world-class works that further enhance the collection.

Following the honour of being awarded Museum accreditation by the government in 1995, the building in Dean Street, London, where the museum had shown for over twenty years, was unexpectedly sold in 1996 and the Ben Uri became homeless. However, following its successful re-launch exhibition *The Ben Uri Story: From Art Society to Museum* in January 2001 in Bond Street, London, the museum finally acquired a new London gallery in St John's Wood in 2002. In partnership with the Jewish Museum, Frankfurt, the Ben Uri celebrated its re-opening in July 2002 with an internationally acclaimed exhibition of works by the German expressionist, Ludwig Meidner, and his artist wife, Else.

Our ongoing and unique series of exhibitions featuring the 'Whitechapel Boys' commenced with Bernard Meninsky in 2001, Mark Gertler in 2002, Jacob Kramer and William Roberts in 2003, Alfred Wolmark in 2004 and continues with *Embracing the Exotic: Jacob Epstein and Dora Gordine* in 2006.

During the past four years, these and other important exhibitions, both historical and contemporary, have seen the Ben Uri re-establish its national and international reputation and blossom into its new identity as The London Jewish Museum of Art.

Our ambition is to spread our message to the largest audience from all communities across the country and abroad, and to move, in the coming years, to a substantial museum and gallery in central London, where, with the benefit of increased exhibition and educational facilities, we will be able to contribute effectively alongside London's other great museums and art institutions.

Selected major exhibitions include:

Sir Jacob Epstein (1980), *Mark Gertler* (1982), *Jacob Kramer* (1984), *Solomon J Solomon RA* (1990), *Abram Games* (1991), *Claude Rogers (1992), Bernard Cohen (1994), The Ben Uri Story* (2001), *Bernard Meninsky* (2001), *Ludwig and Else Meidner* (2002), *Mark Gertler: A New Perspective* (2002), *William Roberts and Jacob Kramer: The Tortoise and the Hare* (2003), *A Storm in Europe: Béla Kádár, Hugó Scheiber and Der Sturm Gallery in Berlin* (2003), *The Modern and the New* (2004), *International Jewish Artist of the Year Competition* (2004), *Alfred Wolmark: a pioneer of British modernism (2004), Abram Games (2005), Chagall and his Circle (2005), Joash Woodrow (2005).*

Registered Museum

Ben Uri Gallery
The London Jewish Museum of Art

Ben Uri Gallery
The London Jewish Museum of Art

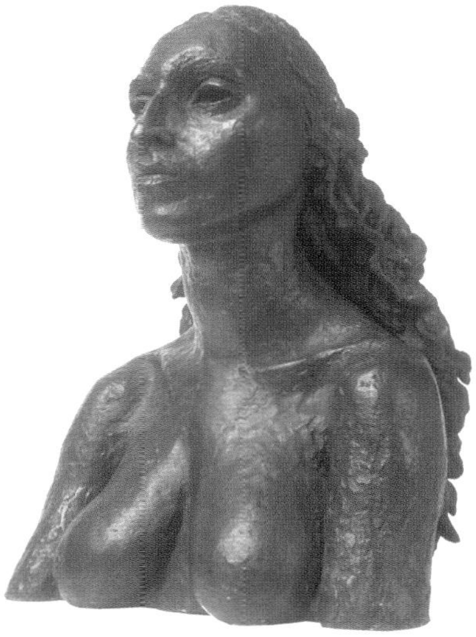

25 Jacob Epstein
Shulamite Woman (Arab Girl), 1935
Ben Uri Collection

108a Boundary Road, London NW8 0RH
Tel: 020 7604 3991 Fax: 020 7604 3992
e-mail: info@benuri.org.uk www.benuri.org.uk

Acknowledgements

This catalogue is published to coincide with the exhibition *Embracing the Exotic: Jacob Epstein and Dora Gordine* at Ben Uri Gallery / The London Jewish Museum of Art 10 January – 19 March 2006, touring to Hatton Gallery, University of Newcastle, 27 March – 20 May 2006

The authors, editors and trustees would like to thank the following for permission to reproduce illustrations:

Plates

Portrait Head of a Young Girl; Genesis II: private collections
Nan (The Dreamer) – head and shoulders; Third Portrait of Meum (Mask); Rani Rama; Illustration for Fleurs du Mal; Nude Study D (Betty Peters): Victor and Gretha Arwas, London
Second Portrait of Lydia; Shulamite Woman (Arab Girl): courtesy of The Ben Uri Gallery, The London Jewish Museum of Art
And the Spirit of God moved upon the Face of the Waters: Birmingham Museum and Art Galleries
Study for Birth: Ivor Braka Ltd, London
Portrait of Nan Condron as the Brummer Head: Private collection, courtesy of Ivor Braka Ltd, London
Study for Man-Woman: The British Museum, London
Chinese Head / Chinaman / Chinese Philosopher; Javanese Dancer; Baby's Head; African Head; Mask of a Greek Boy; Malay Head; Two Women with Earrings; Two Temple Dancers; Standing Nude; Study for Pagan I; Study for Pagan II; Two Oriental Girls; Seated Oriental Woman with Arms Raised; Flawless Crystal; Black Orchid: Dorich House Museum, Kingston University
Self-Portrait; Head of Nan; Study for Tomb of Oscar Wilde; Nan the Dreamer; Study for the Rock Drill; Sunita; Indian Mother and Child; Mask of Nefertiti; Head of Akhenaton; Head of a Bodhisattva (Longmen, Henan Province); Hei-Tiki: Garman Ryan Collection, The New Art Gallery Walsall
One of the Hundred Pillars of the Secret Temple: Private Collection, courtesy of James Hyman Fine Art, London
Study for Figure of Maternity; Seated Figure Study for Rima; Head Study for Rima: Leeds Museums & Galleries (City Art Gallery)
Rom: National Museums and Galleries of Wales
Sun Goddess, Crouching: Nottingham City Museums and Galleries: Nottingham Castle
The Little Negress; Negress; Guadeloupe Head / Negress; Mongolian Head; Javanese Head; A Malay Sultana (The Tungku Ampuan of Johore): © Tate, London, 2005
All Epstein reproductions © Tate, London, 2005

Photographs

Private Collection, courtesy of Ivor Braka Ltd, London: *Portrait of Nan Condron as the Brummer Head*, c.1913.
The British Museum, London: *Colossal Winged Bull from the Palace of Sargon II*, Khorsabad, northern Iraq, Neo-Assyrian, c.710-705 BC; *Sandstone Figure of a Hindu Goddess*, Possibly from Rajasthan, India, 11th century AD, formerly Jacob Epstein collection.
Rachel Dickson: photograph of Betty Peterson, 2005.
Dorich House, Kingston University: *Malay Head*, c.1930-31; *Chinese Head / Kwa Nin (Chinese Lady of Peace)*, c.1930-31; *Javanese Head*, c.1930-31, *Male Torso / Dyak*, c.1930-32; *Pagan*, 1930-32; *Dora Gordine at home* c.1939 (Dorich House Archives); *The Chinese Moon Door at Dorich House with Dora Gordine and Richard Hare at the dining table* (courtesy of Bernard Howarth-Loomes); Dorich House Museum, 2005, (courtesy of Brenda Martin, Dorich House).
Leeds City Art Gallery, Henry Moore Centre for the Study of Sculpture, all formerly Jacob Epstein collection, courtesy of Geoffrey Ireland: *Architectural Carving in form of Male and Female figure, Madagascar; Reliquary Head, Fang, Gabon (The Brummer Head); Head of Lady in Heavy Wig*, Egyptian XV111 18th Dynasty; *Bedroom at Hyde Park Gate showing famous Fang Head and Dogon Mother and Child* c.1959.
Leeds Museums & Galleries (Henry Moore Institute Archive): Jacob Epstein, *Rima, Memorial to W H Hudson*, 1923-5, *The Tomb of Oscar Wilde*, 1909-12, Père Lachaise Cemetery, Paris.
National Portrait Gallery, London: Ida Kar, *Sir Jacob Epstein*, 1953
New Art Gallery Walsall, Garman Ryan Collection: Jacob Epstein, *Baby Awake*, 1902-4.
NMRC / English Heritage: *The Sitting Room at Dorich House in 1949*; *Dorich House*, 1936; *The Gallery at Dorich House*, 1955; *Dora Gordine at work with Richard Hare in the background*, c.1948; *Dora Gordine and Richard Hare having tea on the roof terrace at Dorich House*, c.1948
Private Collection, London: From Wyndham Lewis et al, *Blast no 1: Review of the Great English Vortex* (London: John Lane, 1914); Jacob Epstein Drawing xv, c. 1913-14. Jacob Epstein Drawing xvi, c.1913-14: (photo: Rachel Dickson, 2005).
From Evelyn Silber and Terry Friedman, *Jacob Epstein: Sculpture and Drawings* (Leeds: Maney in association with the Henry Moore Centre for the Study of Sculpture,1987, republished 1989), reproduced p.163 (plate 60): Fig. 10 Jacob Epstein, *Rock Drill*: reconstruction 1973-4 by K Cook and A Christopher after the lost original, 1913-15.
Suzanne Ullman: Dora Gordine, *Susanna*, 1958
The Whitworth Art Gallery, University of Manchester: Jacob Epstein, *Genesis*, 1929-31.

With special thanks to: Miki Slingsby for photography (plates: *Portrait Head of a Young Girl; Nan (The Dreamer) – head and shoulders; Third Portrait of Meum (Mask); Rani Rama; Illustration for Fleurs du Mal; Nude Study D (Betty Peters)* and to all those benefactors, including those who prefer to remain anonymous, who have so generously made this exhibition possible.

The Henry Moore Foundation